THE ILLUSTRATED
HISTORY OF
AMMUNITION

SHELL RIFLED MUZZLE LOADING GUN COMMON
16 INCH   MARK I   § 4115

AVERAGE TOTAL WEIGHT 1700 lb. ± 1·5 PER CENT. BURSTING CHARGE 60 lb.

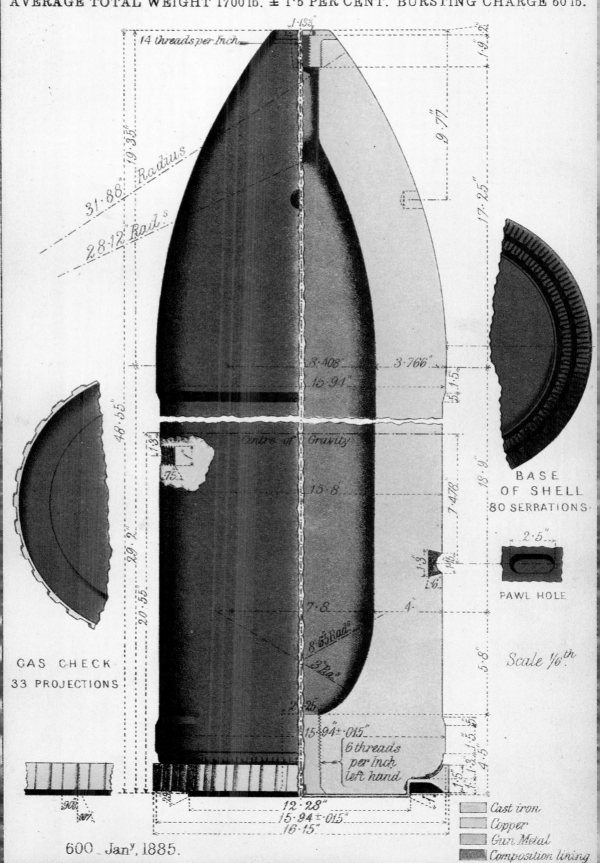

GAS CHECK
33 PROJECTIONS

Centre of Gravity

14 threads per Inch

6 threads per Inch left hand

15·94" ± ·015"

12·28"
15·94" ± ·015"
16·15"

BASE
OF SHELL
80 SERRATIONS

PAWL HOLE

Scale 1/6th.

Cast iron
Copper
Gun Metal
Composition lining

600 — Jan.ʸ 1885.

THE ILLUSTRATED
HISTORY OF
AMMUNITION

Ian V. Hogg

Quantum
Books

A QUANTUM BOOK

This book is produced by
Quantum Publishing Ltd.
6 Blundell Street
London N7 9BH

Copyright ©MCMLXXXV
Quarto Publishing Limited.

This edition printed 2003

ISBN 1-86160-692-3

QUMIHO4

Printed in Singapore by
Star Standard Industries Pte Ltd.

The lead of a Boxer shrapnel shell showing the fuze socket, the wooden head lightly attached to the body of the shell and the central flash tube which is filled with perforated gunpowder pellets to boost the fuze flash down to the expelling charge at the bottom of the shell.

FOREWORD

THERE IS AN OLD SAYING among artillerymen that their weapon is not the gun; it is the shell, and the gun is only the last stage in transportation from the factory to the target. The same applies to all firearms; they are merely devices for discharging bullets, shells, bombs — projectiles of one sort or another — which are the things destined to have the desired effect on the enemy. Without ammunition the finest firearm is merely an expensive club or, at best, a handle for a bayonet, while a piece of artillery with no ammunition is no more than an ornament.

But for all its importance, ammunition is usually taken for granted; received, loaded, fired, and if for some reason it fails to work the firer gets most aggrieved even if he doesn't know why it failed. Yet it is a fascinating subject in its own right. Many a weapon which appeared to have reached the end of its usefulness has been revitalized and given a new lease of life by nothing more than re-designing the ammunition for it, and many weapons have had their effectiveness enhanced by new and improved ammunition. It is impossible to have a complete understanding of a weapon unless there is complete understanding of its ammunition as well.

Although ammunition has been in existence since the first days of firearms in the 14th century, it remained at a fairly static stage of development for the first 400 years. It was not until the Industrial Revolution got into its stride in the mid-19th century that gun design began to show some advances, and with these came improvements in ammunition. The activity of designers and manufacturers in the 1880s and 1890s showed its effect in the South African and Russo-Japanese wars of the early 20th century. These wars led to improvements and innovations which were seen in use during the 1914-18 war, and it was this war which gave ammunition development its greatest impetus to that time. The First World War produced new tactical situations and new techniques of warfare which demanded new types of ammunition. The arrival of military aircraft, for example, brought the first aerial bombs, but it also led to the development of special ammunition for shooting at the aircraft that were dropping these bombs.

The advances made during the First World War were consolidated and refined during the 1920s and 1930s to become the standard ammunition types with which the Second World War was begun. But, once again, advances in military tactics and technology brought new forms of warfare and new types of ammunition. Improvements in the tank brought about improvements in anti-tank projectiles, higher-flying aircraft demanded new types of shell and fuze, portable infantry anti-tank weapons had to be given special projectiles capable of defeating tanks, and so on.

This book cannot, for reasons of space, cover every facet of ammunition; we have, therefore, concentrated on the principal projectile weapons of war — pistols, rifles, machine-guns, mortars, artillery and grenades. We have had to ignore many other interesting areas — mines, torpedoes, aerial bombs and missiles — but the general principles explained in the body of this book apply to every type of ammunition, and with the knowledge gained from these pages it should not be difficult to understand other types of explosive device.

Finally, and for those of a nervous disposition, may I point out that this is not a terrorist's handbook; there are no plans of how to make bombs or any other type of ammunition, and the illustrations are no more explicit than will be found in any encyclopedia or manufacturer's brochure. Nor should anything said in this book be taken as being sufficiently detailed to warrant anyone attempting to dismantle a souvenir; ammunition is designed to kill, and it is entirely colour-blind, taking no note of what uniform, if any, the tampering hand is wearing. So remember: Never tamper with ammunition — it can kill you.

Ian V. Hogg, 1985

FROM CANNON-BALL TO COPPERHEAD

An engraving showing 'Black Berthold', the Mysterious Monk of Freiburg, discovering the principle of the cannon. Charming though this legend may be, there is no evidence that a monk called Berthold Schwartz ever existed. And there is plenty of evidence to suggest that cannon was in use well before the supposed date of his fabled experiment.

Right: The famous *De Officiis Regnum* written by Walter de Milemete. Although there is no mention of firearms in the text, the illustration at the bottom of the manuscript clearly shows a primitive cannon being fired — the touch hole of a bulbous tube, which has an arrow protruding from its muzzle, is being ignited by a man with a hot iron.

ALTHOUGH THE TERM 'ammunition' can be interpreted broadly to cover the stones, prisoners and dead horses flung by catapults into besieged cities in ancient times, the word is usually taken to mean explosive ammunition of some sort, and therefore its history must begin with the first explosive — gunpowder.

Just who invented gunpowder, and where and when, is forever lost in history. At various times it has been credited to the Chinese, the Arabs, possibly even the Lost Tribes of Atlantis, but there is no firm evidence for any of them. The Chinese certainly had pyrotechnic compositions of sorts — fireworks — long before anything of the kind was known in Europe, but this is no warrant for claiming that they invented guns and gunpowder — although for all we know to the contrary they may very well have done.

The first firm signpost on the gunpowder trail can be said to be the publication entitled *De Mirabili Potestate Artis et Naturae* (On the Marvellous Power of Art and Nature), written by Roger Bacon in AD1242. Bacon was a Franciscan monk who prepared several books and papers on philosophical subjects. In this book, at a point in the text where Bacon appears to be skirting the subject of explosives, he includes a string of apparently meaningless words — an aberration that was ignored for centuries, until in the early years of the 20th century a British artillery officer, Colonel Hime, hit upon the answer. The words were an anagram which, when the letters were re-arranged and punctuated, read 'But of saltpetre take seven parts, five of young hazel twig and five of sulphur, and so thou wilt call up thunder and destruction if thou know the art.' If the 'five of young hazel twig' is read instead as charcoal, this provides a workable formula for gunpowder.

But why the anagram? Why not write it plainly for all the world to see and to credit Bacon with, if not the discovery, at least the first announcement of gunpowder? Because Bacon was a monk, and in 1139 the Second Lateran Council had laid under anathema any person who made 'fiery compositions' for military purposes. Had Bacon made an open claim or announcement, he might well have forfeited his life. As it was, due to his outspokenness on various subjects he was removed from his teaching post at Oxford in 1257 and ordered into cloisters in Paris, where he remained out of sight for the next ten years. Then in 1266 he was requested to write a summary of philosophical knowledge for the Pope, after which he was permitted to return to Oxford and resume his teaching.

Among the collection of papers submitted to the Pope was one entitled *Opus Tertius*, a copy of which was discovered in the Bibliothèque Nationale in Paris in 1909. One passage from this makes interesting reading:

> From the flaming and flashing of certain igneous mixtures and the terror inspired by their noise, wonderful consequences ensue which no one can guard against or endure. As a simple example may be mentioned the noise and flame generated by the powder, known in divers places, composed of saltpetre, charcoal and sulphur. When a quantity of this powder no bigger than a man's finger be wrapped in a piece of parchment and ignited, it explodes with a blinding flash and a stunning noise. If a larger quantity were used, or the case made of some more solid material, the explosion would be much more violent and the noise altogether unbearable ... These compositions can be used at any distance we please, so that the operators escape all hurt from them, while those against whom they are employed are filled with confusion..

Bacon makes no claim to having discovered the composition but refers to its use in 'divers places', suggesting that by

1266 the material was common knowledge and he was merely reporting it as a fact.

If we can assume, then, that gunpowder was known to initiates in 1242 and was general knowledge by 1266, the next question to arise is when and where was it first applied to propel something from a gun? (Obviously it could not be called 'gunpowder' until it was used with a gun; exactly what it *was* called in those far-off days is another unsolved mystery.)

There are more spurious claims and legends which must be rapidly dismissed here. One of the most persistent is that of Black Berthold, the Mysterious Monk of Freiburg. Legend says (and is supported by an engraving dated 1643) that one day, experimenting with some powder in a cast-iron vessel, he ignited a charge and thus blew off the lid, and from this deduced the principle of confining a charge in a tube and propelling a shot. A charming legend, but in the first place there is no evidence that Berthold Schwarz ever existed, and in the second place the engraver of the scene gave it a date of 1380, and there is plenty of evidence to show that cannon were in use well before that.

One difficulty is the use of the word 'artillery' in medieval papers; this is often taken to mean 'guns', but the term was in use for many centuries before the gun appeared, in connection with catapults and other engines of war, and its transference to guns went unremarked in the archives. There are various other misleading reports that would be a waste of time to examine. The first positive record, written in AD 1326, reports on the manufacture of brass cannon and iron balls for 'the defence of the commune, camps and territory' of Florence.

Pre-dating this by one year is the famous document *De Officiis Regnum*, written by Walter de Milemete, in which there is an illustration showing the firing of a cannon. The picture is not explained by any text but shows a bulbous tube, with an arrow protruding from the muzzle, being ignited by a man with a hot iron.

From these early records we can see that the first 'ammunition' consisted of the gunpowder used to propel the missile, and either balls or arrows as the missiles them-

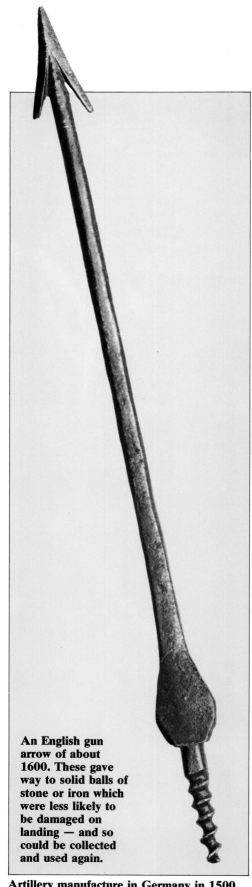

An English gun arrow of about 1600. These gave way to solid balls of stone or iron which were less likely to be damaged on landing — and so could be collected and used again.

Artillery manufacture in Germany in 1500 — Emperor Maximilian and his cannon makers.

The manufacture of gunpowder circa 1450. This engraving shows the material being ground. Note the hourglass. The ingredients had to be ground together for a fixed length of time.

selves. Arrows were well known, and it seems logical that the soldiers of the time would have attempted to adapt the type of missile they knew to the new system of discharge, wrapping a binding of leather around the arrow shaft so as to make it fit tightly into the barrel of the cannon. But making arrows was a skilled business, and using them as cannon projectiles would have been a wasteful affair, so it must have been an obvious step to turn to the use of solid balls, either of stone or cast from iron. These had the advantage that they were unlikely to be damaged on landing and could be salvaged, tidied up, and used again and again (whereas an arrow would probably be damaged beyond repair by a single firing).

Even so, this type of projectile survived for a long time: Sir Francis Drake, in a return to the Government, dated 30 March, 1588, mentions gun-arrows among the stores on his ship.

Stone balls were preferred in the earliest days; indeed, the reference to iron balls in use at Florence is rather remarkable and suggests that the guns were quite small. The argument for this is rather involved, and has to do with the strength and weaknesses of both the guns and the gunpowder. The Milemete drawing shows the cannon in a colour that suggests bronze as the material — a not unreasonable assumption in that the casting of bronze was a well understood art at that time. But it was also expensive, and as the call came for larger cannon, other methods were adopted, notably that of making the barrel from strips of iron bound tightly with straps of metal and rope. Although this was cheaper and easier to make, it was also not as strong as a cast barrel. At the same time, however, the original gunpowder was, by today's standards, weak stuff, so the gun and its powder were more or less well matched. Even so, putting a heavy iron ball into one of these guns and touching off a charge of powder behind it was asking for trouble; the weight of the ball would resist movement so that the explosion of the powder would build up considerable pressure in the gun and might well burst it. A stone ball of the same size would be much lighter — about one-third of the weight of an iron ball — would move

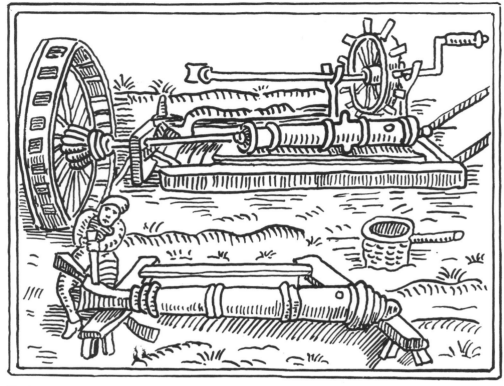

Horizontal gun boring. Foreground — a man is removing the mould after the cannon has been cast. Background — the waterwheel is boring the inside of the barrel.

more quickly, and would thus not allow such a dangerous build-up of pressure.

Another point was that the powder of the day, as well as being weak by formula, was weak by manufacture. Bacon's formula was for 41 per cent saltpetre, 29.5 per cent sulphur and 29.5 per cent charcoal, and doubtless the materials of this day were not to any great degree of purity. Modern gunpowder uses percentage proportions of 75:10:15, together with high standards of purity.

The early powder was mixed by grinding the separate ingredients finely and then mixing them by hand. This dusty mixture was loaded simply by scooping it out of a barrel and pouring it into the gun loosely; there it would settle and consolidate in the chamber with the result that the ignition flame might have difficulty in quickly penetrating through the fine mass to ignite it all at the same time. This led to uncertainty of action, variable power from shot to shot, and also meant that some of the charge was blown out of the muzzle either still burning or unburned — a serious defect

at a time when gunpowder cost a staggering amount, in comparison to the price of iron and lead.

The main drawback with gunpowder was its susceptibility to damp. Saltpetre attracts moisture, and the records of the 14th and 15th centuries are full of complaints about damp powder. It was a very serious problem in that if the powder was unserviceable, the army's teeth were drawn before it got into battle. In 1372-74 there are reports of the purchase of faggots for drying the English powder. Scottish records in 1459 mention keeping powder in waxed cloth bags. Even as late as in 1759 a Royal Navy report of an action off Grenada complained that the shot would not reach the French ships because of damp powder.

Another drawback was that during prolonged travelling, when barrels were being bounced around in carts, the various components of the powder tended to separate, the heavy sulphur sifting through the lighter charcoal. The solution to this problem was generally to carry the three ingre-

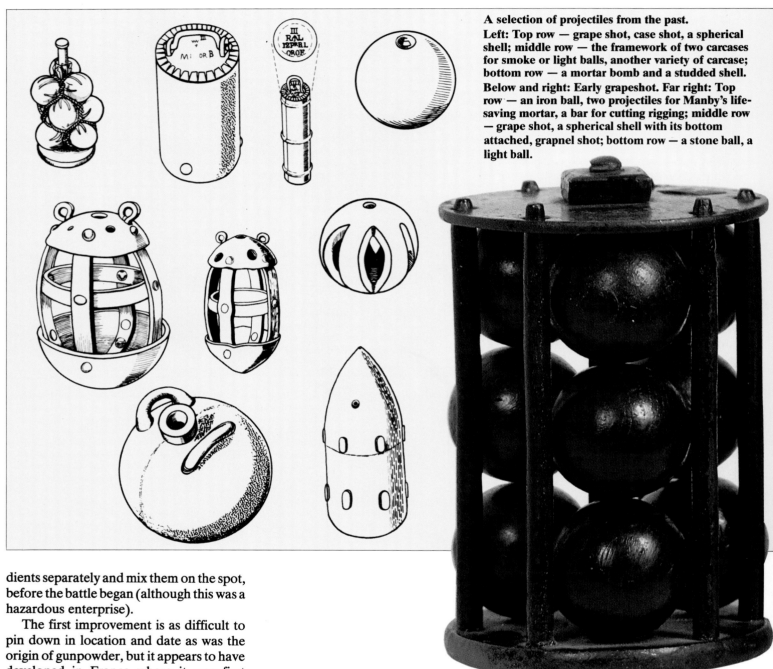

A selection of projectiles from the past.
Left: Top row — grape shot, case shot, a spherical shell; middle row — the framework of two carcases for smoke or light balls, another variety of carcase; bottom row — a mortar bomb and a studded shell.
Below and right: Early grapeshot. Far right: Top row — an iron ball, two projectiles for Manby's life-saving mortar, a bar for cutting rigging; middle row — grape shot, a spherical shell with its bottom attached, grapnel shot; bottom row — a stone ball, a light ball.

dients separately and mix them on the spot, before the battle began (although this was a hazardous enterprise).

The first improvement is as difficult to pin down in location and date as was the origin of gunpowder, but it appears to have developed in France where it was first mentioned in 1429. The improvement was to mix the ingredients in a wet state, which made for better incorporation and less likelihood of accidental explosion, and then to allow it to dry into a cake which was then broken up; the resulting grains were then run through sieves of varying meshes so as to select powder grains for different purposes. The powder was called 'corned powder', and it showed considerable advantages over the original, which then became known as 'serpentine powder'. The granular form allowed flame to penetrate the charge more easily, leading to more certain and regular burning — so much so that corned powder was considered to be about one-third more powerful than the same amount of serpentine. It was also less susceptible to moisture, it no longer separated during transport, and it left a lot less residue and fouling in the bore after firing.

Such is the nature of improvements that these advantages were not attained without some drawbacks. The two principal ones were that corned powder was so powerful it

tended to burst the older guns; and that because of the involved method of manufacture it was even more expensive. As a result it was some time before corned powder gained universal acceptance, but it did have the effect of speeding up the development of cannon, in order that the guns might be strong enough to get the full

benefit from the new powder. Cast-iron cannon began to appear in the middle of the 16th century, and remained the standard pattern for the next 300 years.

Most of the problems with gunpowder centred on the use of saltpetre (potassium nitrate). Until the middle of the 19th century the only source of supply was from

natural deposits, and in Europe these were rare — the material appeared as a surface coating in underground caves, cellars and stables. The major deposits were in the East, and Oriental merchants soon realized the value of their commodity and charged accordingly. In Europe, governments sought to conserve every possible source of supply, so as to reduce their dependence upon the East. In France, 'Saltpetre Commissioners' were appointed in 1540 and had the right of entry into any stable, pigeon-loft, cattle shed or sheep-pen in order to gather saltpetre.

In the early years of the 17th century the East India Company began importing saltpetre into England and built its own gunpowder factory in Surrey. Among the terms for the renewal of the Company's Charter in 1693 was a requirement to supply 500 tons of saltpetre to the Board of Ordnance every year. But merchants had been quick to recognize the profitability of gunpowder many years before that; there was a powder mill in Augsburg in 1340, one in Spandau in 1344. The first powder used by an English army was imported from the continent. This importation continued for many years until the threatening attitude of Spain during Elizabeth I's reign prompted the issue of patents for the manufacture of powder. In 1555 a mill appeared near Rotherhithe, followed by others, and in 1561 a factory was built at Waltham Abbey which grew into the Royal Gunpowder Factory and, in the 20th century, a Royal Ordnance Factory.

The projectile remained the stone or cast-iron ball. The propelling charge was a matter of argument between gunners of the early days, but seems to have been more or less agreed as one-ninth of the weight of the stone shot. As guns increased in strength so the charge was increased to one-fifth or even one-quarter, and this rule was carried over to iron shot, since the difference in weight automatically produced a heavier charge for the heavier projectile.

The only alternative to solid shot was 'langridge', used as an anti-personnel short-range measure. To use 'langridge' simply meant loading a charge and a wad, and then shovelling down the barrel anything and everything which could hurt when fired out again — horse-shoe nails, stones, gravel, scrap metal, flints — anything at all: it was a formidable producer of casualties. Later, the idea of placing this collection into a convenient case was devised, and the result was hence known as 'case shot', which first appears on record during the defence of Constantinople in the middle of the 15th century. An alternative method was to fill a cloth bag with langridge and bind it with cord before loading; this binding caused it to bulge and resemble a bunch of grapes, so that shot in a cloth bag became 'grape shot'.

Ignition of the charge was originally carried out using a hot iron, as evidenced by the Milemete manuscript, but hot irons

Stefan Batory (1533-88), the Polish king responsible for red-hot shot and forming the Cossacks into a militia.

are an inconvenient apparatus to have around the battlefield and a better method soon appeared. The gun was provided with a 'vent' above the chamber into which fine powder was dribbled, to be set off by the hot iron, or by the newly invented alternative, 'quickmatch'. This was simply cord soaked in a solution of saltpetre and then rolled in fine gunpowder and allowed to dry; when ignited it burned very quickly, and a length of this, inserted into the gun vent, proved to be efficient in firing the gun. Unfortunately, it tended to foul the vent, and it became necessary to 'rime' the hole periodically to clean it so that a fresh piece of quickmatch could be used. Some gunners preferred to stick to using fine powder, from their powder horn, because it often found a way past the fouling and reduced the frequency at which riming was needed.

And so, also to replace the hot iron, 'slow match' was devised. This was similar to quickmatch except that it was thicker and dispensed with the gunpowder, so that when lit it merely glowed and burned slowly. It could be revived by blowing on it or whirling it through the air and, attached to a long staff or 'linstock', could be applied to the gun vent.

The first real innovation in projectiles came in 1573 when Master Gunner Zimmermann, a German, invented 'hail shot'. This was a lead cylinder filled half with gunpowder and half with musket balls; a short length of quickmatch passed through a hole in the bottom of the container. As the shot was fired from the gun, so the quickmatch was ignited, burned through and fired the gunpowder inside the casing so that it exploded and blew the musket balls in all directions. This had a range of about a kilometre (600 yards), so that it was a very efficient method of reducing the strength of an opposing army long before it got within hand-to-hand fighting distance.

Very shortly afterwards, in 1579, Stefan Batory, the King of Poland, instituted the use of red-hot shot. Heated balls of clay had often been used with catapults, flung into towns in order to raise fires in the thatched roofs, but the application to guns was slow to come about — which, considering the problems facing the gunners, was not surprising. At first acquaintance the prospect of pushing a red-hot cast-iron ball down on to a charge of gunpowder is not attractive, after all, but Stefan Batory's innovation was firstly to ram a dry wad of cloth down on top of the powder, then a second wad of soaking wet cloth, after which the red-hot ball was tipped into the muzzle and rammed and the gunner touched off the gun as quickly as he could before the hot shot dried out the wet wad.

Solid shot, hot or cold, varied in effect. Against solid targets, such as castles or towns or fortresses, projectiles could do severe damage to the defences. Against individuals on the field of battle they were less reliable — an astute soldier could often see a shot approaching and jump clear, although this was difficult in those days of serried ranks, shoulder-to-shoulder, and with second and third ranks pressing close behind. Moreover, a solid ball did not instantly lose all its energy when it landed; after impact it would often roll and skip for a considerable distance in an erratic manner, retaining sufficient energy to damage anyone it hit. Undoubtedly the gunner's favourite target was a close-packed mass of men, for minor errors in

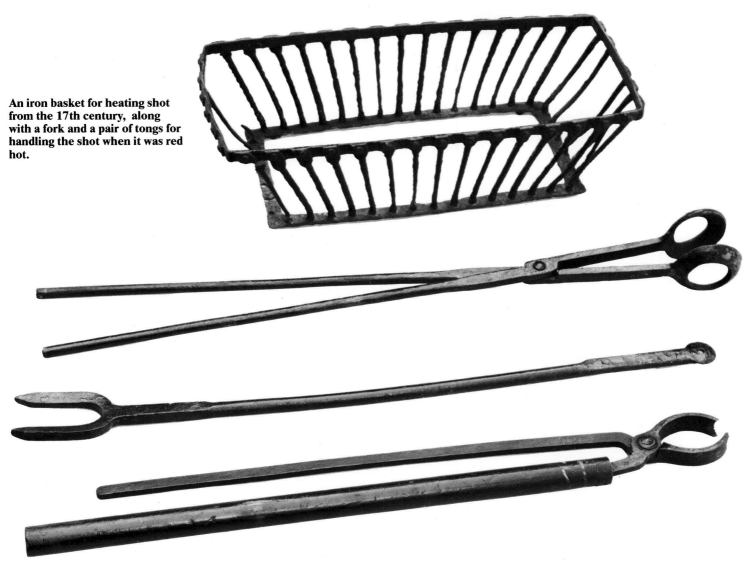

An iron basket for heating shot from the 17th century, along with a fork and a pair of tongs for handling the shot when it was red hot.

aiming, or in the performance of the gun or the powder charge, or in the flight of the ball, would be nullified by the sheer density and vulnerability of the target.

But there were, from the earliest days of artillery, those who sought diligently after a projectile which would contain some explosive effect, and thus have even greater damaging power at the target. Technical problems abounded, however. In the first place the explosive filling had to be set off at the correct place; in the second there was a great danger that the explosive might be jarred into action by the impulse of being shot from the gun, so disposing of the gun and gunners instead of the enemy.

The first moderately successful explosive shells appear to have been fired by the Venetians as early as 1421. The shells were formed of two hollow hemispheres of bronze, joined by a hoop of iron, and with a fuze consisting of a length of quickmatch inside a sheet-iron tube riveted to one of the hemispheres. The interior was filled with a charge of coarse gunpowder. The projectile became known as a *granata* or 'grenade', because the grains of gunpowder were thought to resemble the seeds in a pomegranate. (The word 'shell' appeared later, from the German word *Schall* for 'outside rind or bark'.) This was loaded into a short-barrelled mortar with the fuze against the gunpowder charge so that when the charge was fired to propel the shell, it also lit the fuze. The fuze burned through and, at just about the end of the shell's flight, ignited the gunpowder filling, bursting the shell into fragments.

The business was of course fraught with danger. The construction of the shell was prone to a less than tight joint between the hemispheres, through which the charge's flash could penetrate and burst the shell inside the gun. Or the quickmatch might not thoroughly occupy the iron tube, leaving room for flash to pass down along-side. Or the choice and manufacture of the quickmatch might be faulty so that it flashed down and fired the shell perhaps as it left the muzzle. In any event, the result was unpopular with the gunners and shells never became common as an article of war in the 15th century.

It was not until the 17th century that shells became popular in Europe. The reason for the delay was simply that a shell was not a practical device without an accurate fuze, and there could not be an accurate fuze until there was an accurate and convenient method of measuring short intervals of time. When the first practical watches appeared, in the 1670s, the problem was at last amenable to solution.

The fuzes developed for shells were simple enough devices: tapered cylinders of beech wood (chosen for its hardness and impermeable grain) through which a central hole was bored and filled with a composition of gunpowder and 'spirits of

Muzzle-loading shells with bronze studs angled to the gun's rifling pitch.

wine' — alcohol. This, rammed in to a suitable density, burned relatively slowly, and the wooden body of the fuze was marked off in distances. The fuze was physically cut off at the appropriate distance by means of a knife, and then driven into a hole in the shell; when fired, the flash from the charge lit the exposed outer end of the train of gunpowder, which then burned through until it lit the filling of the shell. Interestingly the expression 'to cut a fuze' is still in use with some artillery forces to this day, even though the setting of the modern fuze is achieved by a totally different method.

The method of igniting the fuze still posed problems. Loading the shell with the fuze towards the charge was one way; another was to use a gun with two vents, one to ignite the fuze and the other to ignite the charge (a rare system, as might be imagined); and a third was to load the shell with the fuze towards the muzzle and then, shortly before firing, reach down through the muzzle with a length of slow match and ignite the fuze. (It can be appreciated that this latter system was far from popular with the unfortunate who was to do the lighting.) But in about 1740 some unknown genius suddenly realized that there was enough air-space around the shell to permit it to be loaded with the fuze towards the muzzle and still be lit efficiently by the charge flame washing around the shell. That there was such space followed from the necessity for the shell to be slightly smaller than the bore of the gun in order that during ramming air would not be trapped underneath it. And where air could escape, flame could pass. And so 'single fire' became the vogue in the mid-18th century.

Another desirable effect which inventors pursued was the use of incendiary materials in shells, both to ignite material and also to provide illumination during night-time warfare. Various expedients were tried with little or no success until the 'carcass' was invented in 1672, reputedly by a Master Gunner in the service of Christopher van Galen, the Prince-Bishop of Münster. The carcass was a spherical iron framework wrapped in cloth and cord and filled with a mixture of saltpetre,

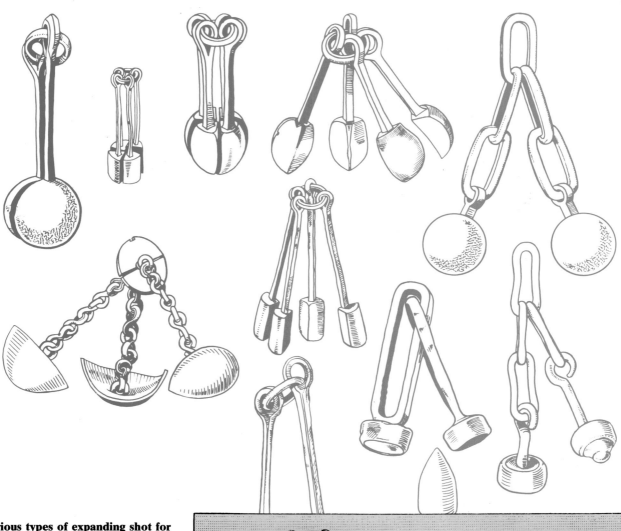

Above: Various types of expanding shot for cannon used particularly by naval guns for cutting rigging.

Above right: An early light ball. The fuze is coiled around the body and burns in flight.

Right: An early type of grenade which was thrown by means of a rope.

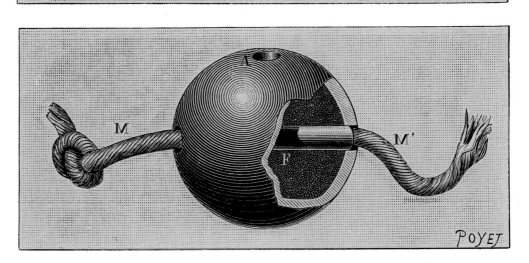

sulphur, Venetian turpentine, tallow and resin. This villainous compound, ignited by the normal type of fuze, would then burst asunder, scattering the flaming liquid in all directions; because of its composition it would stick to surfaces and ignite them too, proving very difficult to fight with nothing more sophisticated than water. The only drawback in practice was the fact that in order to get the maximum filling into each carcass, the construction was somewhat flimsy; unless precautions were taken it was all too possible for them to burst in the bore of the gun through the shock of the

Casting cannon balls circa 1800. The man on the right is cutting off the cast marks to make the cannon ball round.

charge being fired behind them. As a result, it was normal to reduce the charge and pack a thick wad of turf or some similarly absorbent substance on top of the charge to act as a damper between the explosion and the carcass.

A variant of the carcass which also appeared in the 17th century was the 'smoke ball' which, according to a contemporary document, 'during their combustion cast forth a noisome smoke and that in such abundance that it is impossible

to bear it'. In view of the contents of the smoke ball — saltpetre, coal, pitch, tar, resin, sawdust, crude antimony and sulphur — this seems a valid claim, and probably marks it as the forerunner of chemical warfare.

And so, with the artillerymen amply supplied with gunpowder and their assortment of projectiles, let us leave them for a while and go back again to the 14th century to trace the second line of development: ammunition for hand weapons.

The cannon came first; the 'hand-gonne' came some time afterwards and was simply a shrunken version of the contemporary cannon that was mounted on a wooden stave which could be tucked under the firer's arm to give support and some direction to the weapon. The design was gradually refined to a more manageable size, and split into two — the shoulder arm and the hand gun — each of which passed through stages of development without moving from the muzzle-loading concept.

The breech of an early breech-loading gun which belonged to Henry VIII.

These three musketeers are carrying arquebuses complete with serpentine locks. This development allowed the gunman to hold the firearm firmly with both hands while firing.

The history of small-arms ammunition during the period is relatively meagre in that it is simply the history of lead balls and gunpowder, neither of which changed very much once the definitive forms had been arrived at in the 16th century. The only important change lay in the method of ignition which, properly, is a matter for the history of the gun and not of the ammunition. Nevertheless that history does eventually lead into the sphere of ammunition, and an understanding of the problem is necessary in order to understand why a solution was so desirable.

The first small arms took the contemporary method of firing a cannon and extended it; the 'hand-gonner' tucked the stave under his arm, aimed — one way or another, since in those days there were no such things as sights — and touched a burning slow match to the vent, which he had primed with gunpowder. Experience soon showed that it was desirable to be

gripping the weapon with both hands when it went off, and very quickly the 'serpentine lock' was invented: simply a Σ-shaped piece of metal pivoted on the stave, with the forward end holding the match and the rear end in a convenient place to be pulled by the firer so as to lower the match to the vent while he held the gun securely.

The serpentine lock was refined into the matchlock, in which the apparatus was fixed to a small plate at the side of the gun and controlled by a spring and catch. The

arm holding the match was pulled back and retained, against a spring, by a stud which was released by being pushed by the firer, so that the match flew forward on to the vent. Since the lock was at the side, it made sense to alter the vent so that it too came out at the side of the barrel and ended in a pan into which loose powder could be sprinkled. At the same time the form of the weapon changed: the barrel became longer and a shoulder stock appeared, generally taking on the form that is recognized today.

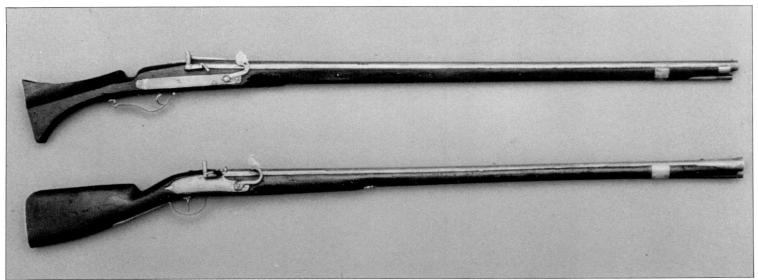

Two 17th century English matchlock muskets. The top one was made about 1630, the bottom one in 1690.

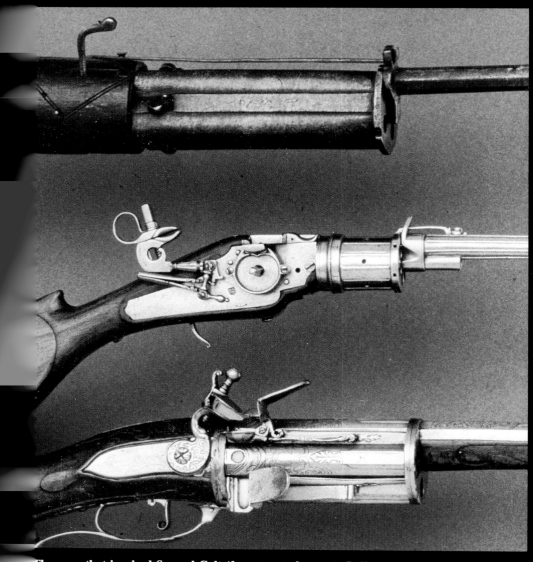

The guns that inspired Samuel Colt (from top to bottom): Indian matchlock, wheellock, flintlock, short musket of 1770.

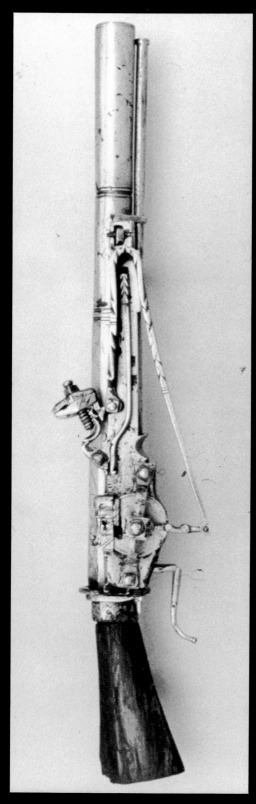

An Italian pistol originating from about 1520. It uses an early wheellock design. Note the unguarded trigger.

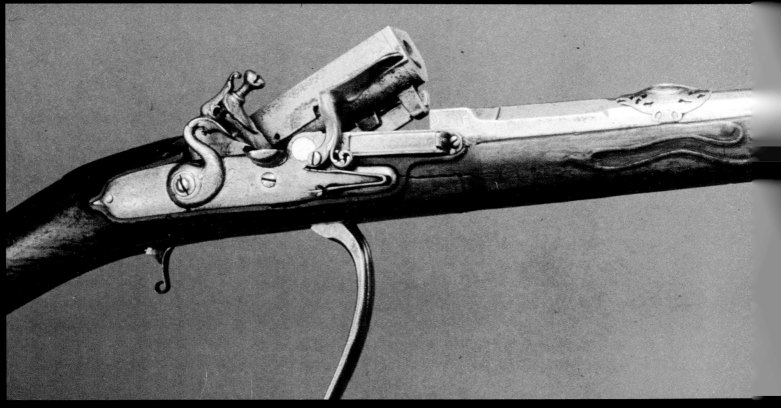

Above: A flintlock breech-loader by Birchell.

Below: Early repeating rifles with sliding locks.

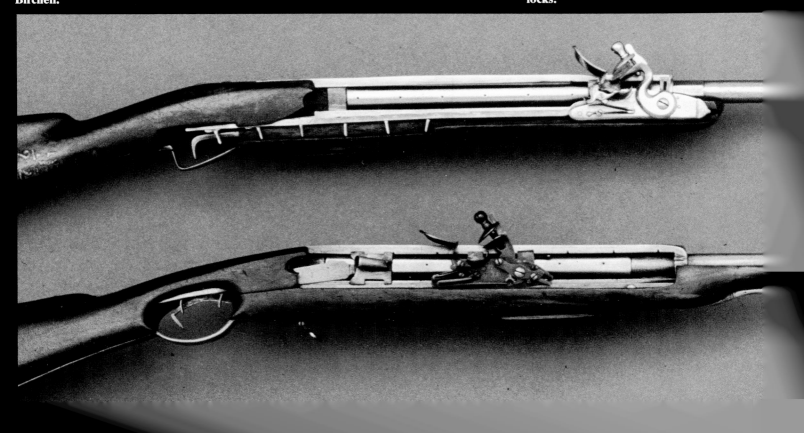

Reverend Alexander Forsyth who developed the first percussion system in 1805.

After the matchlock came the wheel-lock, invented in about 1500, which uses a roughened wheel, driven by a spring which had first to be wound up or 'spanned'. When the trigger was pulled the wheel spun, its surface in contact with a piece of flint, so that sparks were directed into the pan of powder.

About 50 years later the flintlock appeared (first called the 'snap-lock'). By this mechanism a flint was securely held in the jaws of the 'cock' and allowed to move forward, when released by the trigger, to strike a carefully positioned piece of steel and so produce the requisite sparks. With later minor refinements this was the height of technical development in small-arms ammunition systems, and it remained the only method of ignition until the 19th century.

All these systems were clumsy and prone to accident. The pan was fitted with a lid fairly early in its development — an endeavour to keep out damp and prevent the loose powder from being blown away or otherwise dislodged. The pan cover later formed the steel on which the flint struck, so that the blow performed two functions, generating a spark and throwing open the pan to expose the powder. Indeed, the whole business of loading was wide open to accidents: the powder had to be sifted down the barrel; the ball inserted and rammed; a wad rammed on top to prevent it from falling out again or rolling away from the powder; loose powder had to be sprinkled into the pan and vent; the flint had to be prepared correctly and properly set into the jaws of the cock ... It was remarkable that the firearms worked at all.

One constant factor in flintlock weapons was the appreciable pause between pulling the trigger and the gun actually going off. Watch a flintlock being fired and it is possible to distinguish the separate events; first the flint ignites the pan and then, a fraction of a second later, the discharge of the gun itself follows. If such a delay was inconvenient for soldiers, it was positively traumatic for sportsmen. At the first flash of the flint and pan many a quarry would take fright and flee often far enough during the pause to escape the line of fire entirely (particularly if the gunner's aim had been poor in the first place).

It was this irritating characteristic of the flintlock gun which led the Reverend Alexander Forsyth, Minister of Belhelvie in Scotland, to devote much of his life to developing a better method of igniting the powder charge. In 1805 he developed the first percussion system, using a mixture of mercury fulminate and potassium chlorate which, when struck with a falling hammer, detonates and gives off a strong flash. By replacing the cock of the flintlock with a hammer, and arranging for a small measure of powder to be dropped at the mouth of the 'vent' leading into the gun chamber, Forsyth produced a system that was practically instantaneous. He offered the idea to the Board of Ordnance, but in 1807 they turned it down. Forsyth duly patented it and, in conjunction with the famous gunsmith James Purdey, began to produce percussion sporting guns. In 1842, after much wrangling, he was awarded £200 by the Board of Ordnance, who had by now appropriated the idea for their own use. After his death in 1843 an additional sum of £1,000 was distributed among his dependants.

Various mechanisms for containing and placing the igniting powder were tried; the

A double-barrelled percussion shotgun made by le Page Moutier of Paris which was shown at the 1862 exhibition at South Kensington.

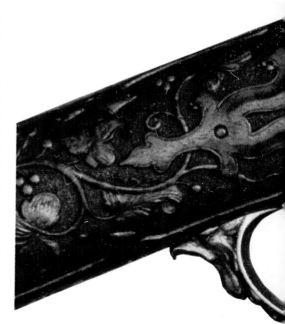

system evolved that was eventually regarded as the best was to place the powder in a tiny copper cap, rather like a miniature top hat. Pressed carefully into the 'crown' of the hat and secured there with a dab of varnish, it was waterproof and could not fall out. The vent of the gun was then finished off with a screwed-in hollow tube, called the 'nipple', which was in line with the hammer. The cap was placed, open end down, on the nipple so that when the hammer was released it fell, crushing the cap and the powder and thus forcing the flash to drive down the vent and into the gun chamber to ignite the powder charge.

By 1840 the percussion system had almost entirely replaced the flintlock. The British Army adopted it in 1838, the Americans in 1842, and by that time almost every other army had also taken to it. In the sporting world its adoption was even faster, and it is safe to say that by 1845 the number of flintlocks still in use was negligible. Many gunsmiths made a good living by converting flintlocks to percussion, merely fitting a hammer and nipple in place of the cock and pan, since the rest of the gun remained the same.

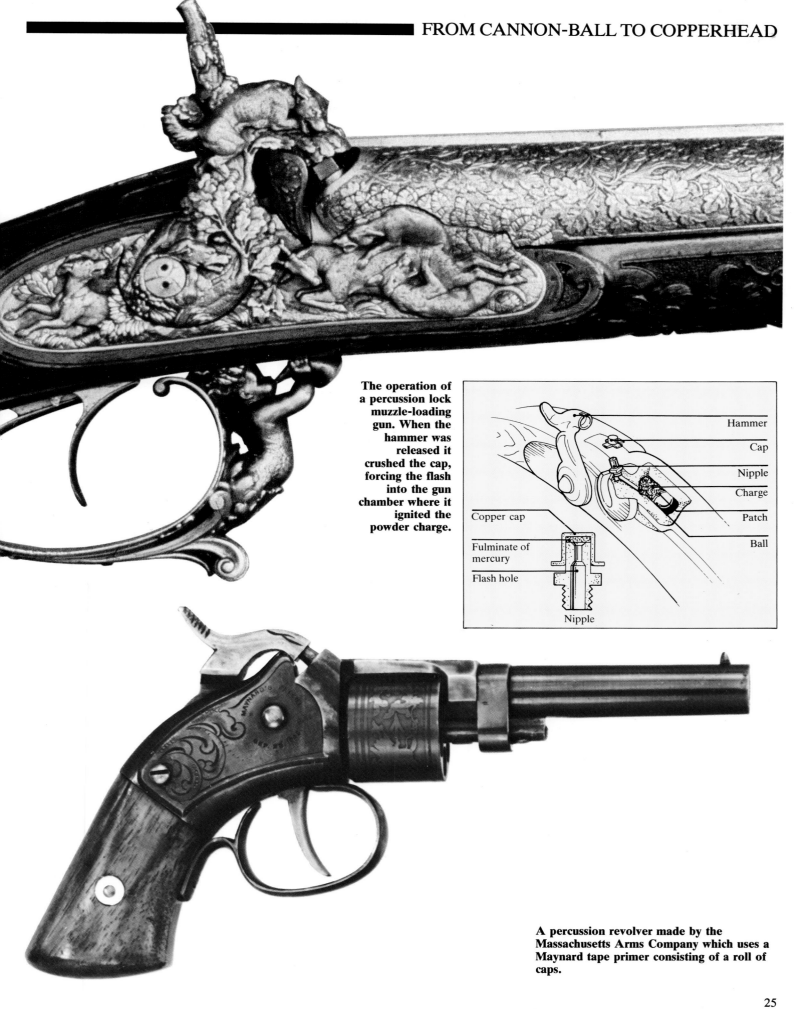

The operation of a percussion lock muzzle-loading gun. When the hammer was released it crushed the cap, forcing the flash into the gun chamber where it ignited the powder charge.

Hammer

Cap

Nipple

Charge

Patch

Ball

Copper cap

Fulminate of mercury

Flash hole

Nipple

A percussion revolver made by the Massachusetts Arms Company which uses a Maynard tape primer consisting of a roll of caps.

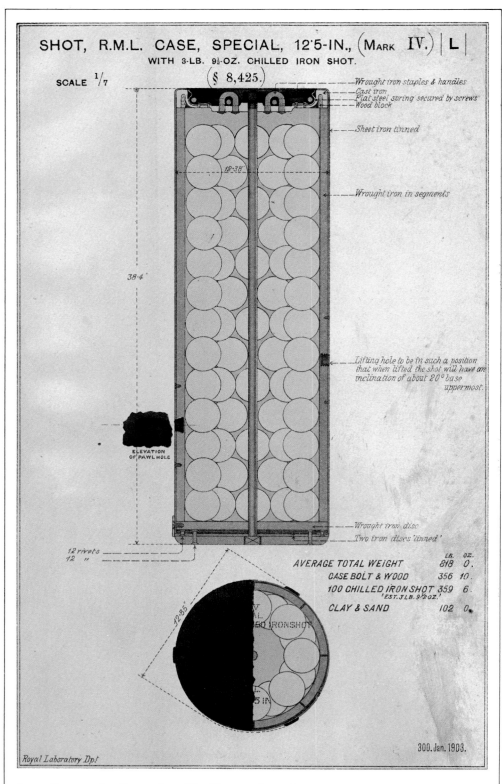

SHOT, R.M.L. CASE, SPECIAL, 12·5-IN., (Mark IV.) | L |
WITH 3-LB. 9¼-OZ. CHILLED IRON SHOT.
(§ 8,425.)
SCALE ¹/₇

Wrought iron staples & handles
Cast iron
Flat steel spring secured by screws
Wood block

Sheet iron tinned

12·38"

Wrought iron in segments

38·4"

Lifting hole to be in such a position
that when lifted the shot will have an
inclination of about 20° base
uppermost.

ELEVATION
OF PAWL HOLE

Wrought iron disc
Two iron discs 'tinned'

12 rivets
12 ,,

12·85"

IRONSHOT

5 IN

	LB.	OZ.
AVERAGE TOTAL WEIGHT	818	0.
CASE BOLT & WOOD	356	10.
100 CHILLED IRON SHOT	359	6.
'EST. 3 LB. 9½ OZ.'		
CLAY & SAND	102	0.

300. Jan. 1903.

Royal Laboratory Dpt.

An early example of case shot. The diagram shows how the shot was packed.

So convenient a method of priming the weapon demanded an equally convenient method of loading, and by this time the casual sprinkling of powder down the muzzle had largely been overtaken by pre-formed cartridges, particularly for military use. The cartridge was a tube of paper containing the correct powder charge and the ball. To load, the paper was torn open and the powder emptied down the barrel; the paper was then crumpled and forced down on top of the powder as a retaining wad, making certain that no matter how the gun was manipulated the powder remained in the chamber and adjacent to the ignition system; the ball was thrust into the muzzle and rammed; the hammer cocked and a cap replaced on the nipple; and the weapon was ready to fire.

The spherical lead ball that had been the standard projectile for hand weapons since their introduction had certain defects. The biggest one was that it was directionally inaccurate. In order that the ball could be forced down the barrel it had to be of smaller diameter than the inside of the bore of the weapon. When fired, it thus tended to bounce from side to side as it went up the barrel, and its final direction depended largely upon which side of the barrel it bounced off last. In flight it was retarded by the air through which it passed, and because it was the same size viewed from any angle (it was not in any way aerodynamic), the effect of wind was totally random, there being no inbuilt stabilizing factor. The fault had been realized for many years, and there had been periodic attempts to improve matters.

The most usual method was to rifle the barrel of the gun; by cutting a series of spiral grooves in the bore it was possible to make the ball spin, and this gave it gyroscopic stability which tended to keep it on a constant path. In order to make the ball grip the rifling, however, it had now to be slightly bigger than the diameter across the raised part of the rifling (known as the 'lands'). To load the ball it had to be hammered down, engraving into the rifling as it went, so that it would ride in the grooves as it left. Such hammering usually deformed the soft lead ball, with the result that any accuracy gained from the rifling

Early spherical case shot or shrapnel. These were little more than hollow cannon balls filled with lead balls and a small central burster charge of gunpowder.

was generally lost due to the battered shape of the ball as it flew through the air.

The obvious solution was to arrange things so that the ball was below bore diameter as it went in but was somehow expanded to slightly greater diameter before it left. Achieving this aim brought forth some peculiar stratagems. One of the earliest systems was to have an upstanding pillar in the breech end of the barrel; when the ball was dropped in it stopped on the tip of this pillar, the powder of the charge being distributed around the pillar and under the ball. A few sharp blows with the ramrod then caused the ball to be driven against the pillar and expand outwards so that it bit into the rifling. When fired, the ball was engaged in the rifling and flew quite well.

It then occurred to some experimenters that the explosion of the charge might be used to do the expanding, if the shape of the bullet were altered. And so, for the first time, a cylindrical bullet with a pointed nose was employed. The base of this bullet was hollowed out to leave a relatively thin 'skirt' and the hollow filled with a hard metal cone. Loaded, the bullet slipped down inside the rifling and came to rest on the powder charge and wad in the usual way. When the charge was fired the sudden eruption of gas pressed on the metal cone, which in turn pressed on the soft lead skirt and forced it outwards into the rifling as the

Right: a spherical shrapnel shell. The bursting charge is separated from the bullets by a thin metal diaphragm. Note that the wooden base holds the boxer fuze at the top, away from the propelling charge.

Below right: a cartridge for a muzzle-loading rifle using an expanding 'Minié' bullet.

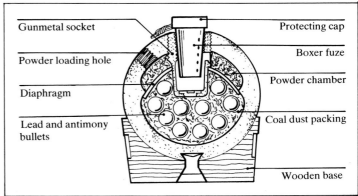

Gunmetal socket — Protecting cap
Powder loading hole — Boxer fuze
Diaphragm — Powder chamber
Lead and antimony bullets — Coal dust packing
Wooden base

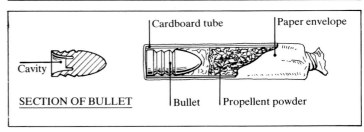

Cavity
SECTION OF BULLET
Cardboard tube | Paper envelope
Bullet | Propellent powder

bullet gathered speed. The 'cylindro-conoidal' shape gave better flight characteristics, and this 'Minié Bullet' — named after its promoter rather than its inventor — was soon adopted for military use all over the world. The British Army tried it but objected to the metal cup: it was too expensive, too fiddling to manufacture and, if the truth were known, probably would have involved paying a patent fee. So the British adopted a bullet of their own which resembled the Minié in principle but

used a far simpler method of expanding the base: a solid clay plug, which, impelled by the gases, achieved the expansion just as well as the expensive metal cone and did far less damage to the rifle barrel.

By the 1850s, therefore, the infantry of the major armies were armed with a rifled muzzle-loading musket which could deliver a heavy ball — usually of about .5-inch calibre — with considerable accuracy out to quite long ranges. This brought about something of a revolution on the bat-

27

tlefield. For the first time it became possible for infantry to out-range artillery; the smoothbore guns of the day showed little improvement over those of two centuries before, but the rifle had made great strides, and the cannon was no longer the master of the battlefield. Guns brought into action in full view of the enemy perhaps 450 metres (500 yards) away, as had been the tactical principle for years, were at considerable risk, since the enemy infantry could shoot the gunners a good deal more easily than the gunners could deal with the mass of infantry. The time had come to make some fundamental changes in artillery.

There was just one item of ammunition which prevented complete disaster for the artillery of the time, and that was the shrapnel shell, named after its inventor Colonel Henry Shrapnel.

This projectile had been developed as a method of killing infantry at long range with more certainty than a solid cannonball could offer. In the Siege of Gibraltar towards the end of the 18th century a Captain Mercier had experimented with firing mortar shells from a suitably sized howitzer; fitted with a short fuze and fired with a reduced charge these shells burst in the air over the enemy infantry, showering them with splinters.

After the siege, Shrapnel (then a lieutenant) set about improving on the idea, and in 1784 he produced his 'spherical case shot'. This was a thin iron ball containing a filling of musket balls and gunpowder; a wooden fuze was inserted and when it burned through it ignited the gunpowder which then exploded to shatter the casing and blow the musket balls in all directions. Shrapnel's idea was to 'extend the range of case shot' by allowing the projectile to get to the enemy before it burst, so that he reproduced the effect of case shot but took it from the gun muzzle and placed it among the enemy.

The whole point about Shrapnel's development is that he did not simply cram as much gunpowder as possible into the shell in order to obtain a powerful blast. The amount of gunpowder was deliberately kept low so that all it did was open up the shell — the balls obtained their velocity from the forward motion of the

A typical example of case shot, sectioned to show its constituent parts.

shell at the time of the burst. After many tests and trials it was formally approved in 1792, but it remained known as 'spherical case shot' until it was officially renamed 'Shrapnel shell' in 1852 in memory of its inventor.

Apart, though, from shrapnel the artillery had few means of overcoming the new superiority of the infantry. The gunmakers therefore urgently began to look at methods of rifling a cannon and, more important, of developing suitable projectiles. There was no possibility of using the expansive properties of lead, as did the shoulder arms. Ideas had been put forward from time to time in the past: in 1821 Lieutenant Croly of the 1st Regiment of Foot had suggested rifling the gun barrel and using a lead-coated ball; a similar idea was later put forward by the Swedish Baron Wahrendorff in 1846; in 1842 a Frenchman, Cavalier Treulle de Beaulieu, had suggested a cannon with deep grooves and with studs on the shell to ride in the grooves; and in 1845 a Major Cavalli of the Sardinian Army had proposed a gun rifled with two grooves and a shell having two ribs to match. Although some desultory tests were made of these various ideas, nobody took them particularly seriously until the Crimean War in 1854. Then money suddenly became available and soldiers began to show some interest, especially when confronted with long-range infantry fire. The British Government took the decision to provide a number of guns rifled according to an idea by Henry Lancaster, an English gunmaker. Lancaster's idea was to make a gun with an oval bore which was twisted; the projectile was oval in section and had opposite sides planed on the skew so as to match the twist of the bore.

The guns were not a success. The shot showed a tendency to jam in the bore, either on loading or firing, damaging the bore as a result, and the already poor accuracy rapidly worsened. They were soon withdrawn from service and the Army cast around for a better idea.

One was provided by a Mr William Armstrong, a solicitor from Newcastle-on-Tyne, who had a controlling interest in an engineering company. Appalled by reports from the Crimea which highlighted the great difficulties involved in moving an 18-pounder (weighing three tons, or 3,000kg) through the mud at of Inkerman, Armstrong sat down and designed a totally new type of gun, his object being primarily to save weight and distribute what weight there was in a more scientific manner. At the same time, he introduced the concept of loading the gun from the breech end rather than from the muzzle, rifled it, and developed a new type of ammunition.

The details of Armstrong's system of gun manufacture is less significant to this historical outline than the manner of loading, which was both revolutionary and very important for future developments. The rear end of the barrel terminated in a sort of box, open at top and bottom and with a threaded hole in the rear end opposite the entrance to the barrel — or the 'chamber' as the rear end was now called. The projectile was loaded in through the hole, followed by the propelling charge — a bag of gunpowder — and then a slab of steel called the 'vent piece' was dropped into the top of the box to close the rear of the chamber. It was then jammed tightly against the chamber, so as to make a gas-tight fit, by putting a large screw through the hole in the 'box' and winding it tight. The face of the vent piece had a copper plate which helped to make an effective seal to prevent the gas leaking out when the cartridge was fired.

Firing was carried out by having a hole in the vent piece and using a 'friction igniter', a goose-quill filled with powder and with a topping of phosphorus compound. A jagged piece of metal passed through the compound and when this was jerked free the roughness ignited the phosphorus — a system analogous to a common match being struck on a rough surface — and the powder was fired, shot flame down the vent, and fired the cartridge.

The gun was rifled with several shallow grooves. The projectile was coated with a layer of lead; moreover, it was more or less shaped as shells are today — a cylinder with a rounded nose. The shell sat in the smoothbored chamber and when it was exploded into movement by the powder charge the lead coating bit into the rifling, which began just in front of the rest position, and the shell left the barrel

Above: Sir William Armstrong, the inventor of the breech-loading gun.

Below: The mechanism of the Armstrong rifled breech-loading cannon.

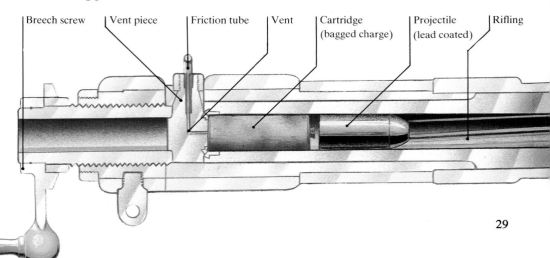

Breech screw | Vent piece | Friction tube | Vent | Cartridge (bagged charge) | Projectile (lead coated) | Rifling

Left: *Gloire*, the first French ironclad whose construction forced the development of heavy artillery in Britain.

Right: A friction igniter — an improvement on the early goose-quill type. Here a copper tube is used instead.

Below: The British response to the *Gloire* was the *Warrior*. This was the first British ironclad.

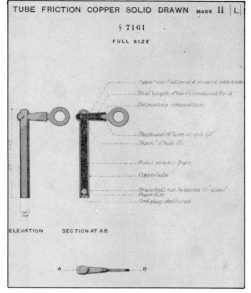

TUBE FRICTION COPPER SOLID DRAWN MARK II L.

§ 7161

FULL SIZE

ELEVATION   SECTION AT A B

spinning. This gave the Armstrong gun remarkable accuracy in comparison with any other cannon, and it also meant that the shell arrived at the target point-first, unlike a cannon-ball which might be in any attitude when it arrived. Armstrong rounded off this technical *tour de force* by inventing a time fuze, one which relied on a length of gunpowder and could be adjusted by simply twisting a brass cap to set an arrow against various figures engraved on the body of the fuze.

Several thousand Armstrong guns were built for the British Army and Navy between 1855 and 1865 — but then came a sudden reversion to muzzle-loading, which has frequently been held up as an example of British resistance to modern innovation. In fact, it was a reasoned response to a

Armstrong lead-coated shells — on the right the lead has been removed to show the retaining notches.

difficult problem the British Navy now faced.

The French Navy had caused the problem by launching the world's first ironclad warship and compounded it by uttering belligerent noises even as Napoleon III began talking of enlarging the French empire. The British Navy immediately replied by setting about building ironclads of their own, but the pressing problem was to find guns capable of defeating these armoured ships. A 68-pounder smoothbore, provided with a special hardened steel shot, could just about manage to penetrate the iron armour at short range. But such a tactic was no solution because the French ships, which were largely armed with shell-firing guns, would reduce the wooden British warships to shattered wrecks before much impression had been made on their own armour. The Armstrong gun, efficient as it was, was weak in its breech closing and thus unable to withstand a powerful enough charge to send a penetrating shot with sufficient velocity to smash the armour. The only solution was to go back to massive muzzle-loading guns that could take heavy charges and fire potent projectiles at high velocity.

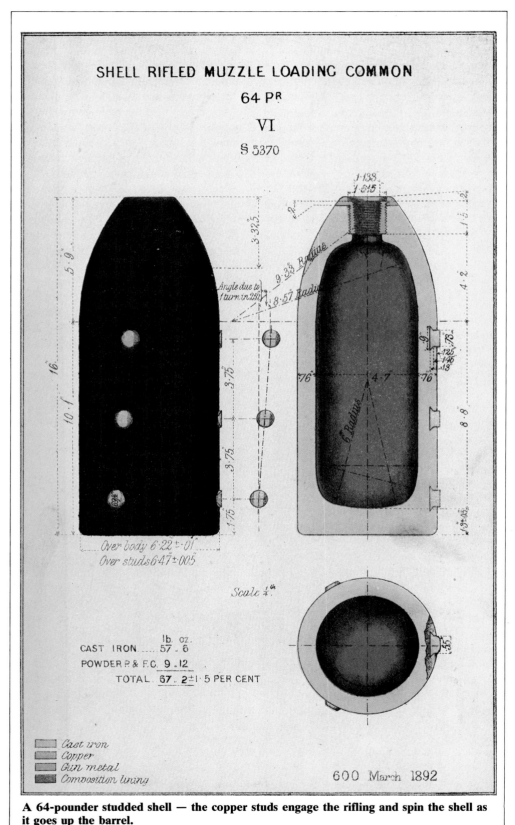

SHELL RIFLED MUZZLE LOADING COMMON

64 P^R

VI

S 5370

Over body 6·22 ± ·01"
Over studs 6·47 ± ·005"

Scale ¼ th

	lb.	oz.
CAST IRON	57	6
POWDER P. & F.C.	9	12
TOTAL	67	2 ± 1·5 PER CENT

Cast iron
Copper
Gun metal
Composition lining

600 March 1892

A 64-pounder studded shell — the copper studs engage the rifling and spin the shell as it goes up the barrel.

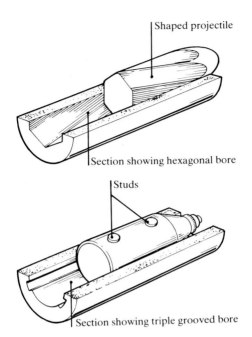

Shaped projectile

Section showing hexagonal bore

Studs

Section showing triple grooved bore

The rival rifling systems to impart spin to muzzle-loading projectiles. Above: The Armstrong. Top: The Whitworth.

It so happened that a suitable design was ready to hand. In 1863 another British manufacturer, Joseph Whitworth, had offered a new system of rifling in which, again, the bore was actually smooth but was hexagonal and with a twist in it. The projectile was likewise hexagonal, the sides being angled so as to match the angle of twist. He objected to the Armstrong monopoly of providing British guns and demanded a comparative trial; a Whitworth muzzle-loader, an Armstrong breech-loader and an Armstrong muzzle-loader were selected for competition, and the Armstrong muzzle-loading system was adjudged best. The Armstrong muzzle-loader used three deep grooves in the barrel and three rows of soft metal studs on the shell; the studs were introduced into the grooves as the shell was entered into the muzzle, rode down as the shell was rammed, and then rode up the grooves again, spinning the shell as it was fired. It was simple and reliable, whereas Whitworth's system, like the similar Lancaster, jammed its shot too often for comfort. And so the Armstrong breech-loading gun was quietly retired, and the RML (rifled muzzle-loader) came in its place.

Whatever the system, one thing was certain; the day of the cannon-ball was over, and the elongated shot or shell was now the rule. But actually perfecting elongated shot and shell to perform in the way the soldiers wanted was a slow business and led to some long and expensive trials. And yet, as is often the case, the best ideas came from outside the mainstream of ammunition development; an example is the piercing shot adopted in Britain.

The prime demand in the late 1860s was for something to go through 60 centimetres (24 inches) or so of wrought iron armour supported by a foot or more of solid teak wood, which was the accepted method of construction of the early ironclad ships. Cast iron had been the normal material for making cannon-balls, and it had carried over into Armstrong's shells, but cast iron flung against a wrought iron shield simply shattered. Attempts were made to construct steel shells, but steel-making was still something of an infant art in the 1860s, not entirely understood and not capable of regularly producing flawless billets from which shot could be made. Moreover, of course, steel was expensive.

What complicated the issue was that there were two schools of thought on the question of how to defeat armour: the 'racking' and the 'punching' schools. The 'rackers' wanted to fire a big heavy projectile at low velocity and thus 'rack' or strain the entire structure of the armour so as to bring about its collapse and expose the interior of the ship. The 'punchers' wanted high-velocity light shot which could punch through the plate so that both it and the fragments of armour it displaced would act as projectiles to do damage behind the armour. In short, the rackers were out to destroy the armour and the punchers were after whatever the armour was protecting. To a great extent the punchers were proved right and the rackers wrong, but their argument led in the meanwhile to a lot of time-wasting on the theory of flat-headed and round-headed projectiles.

As all this was going on, a Captain Palliser of the 18th Hussars — a regiment not noted at that time for scientific application — devised a pointed projectile which he cast with its nose down in a water-cooled

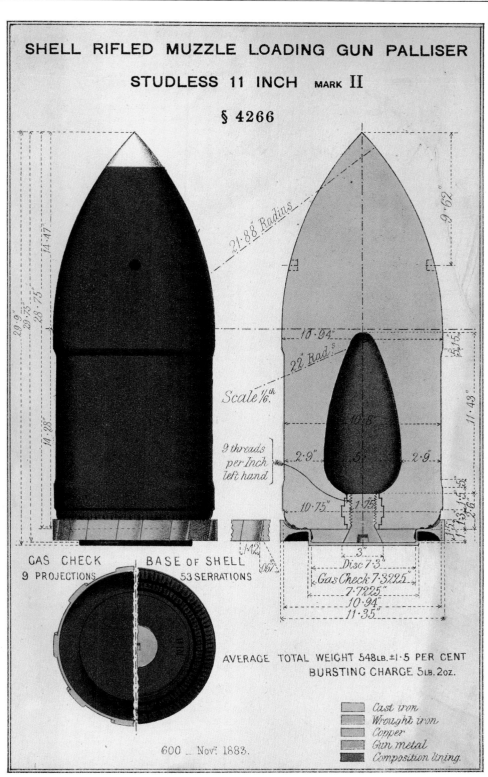

An 11in Palliser shell. The tip was cast nose-down in a water-cooled iron mould which made the point extremely hard.

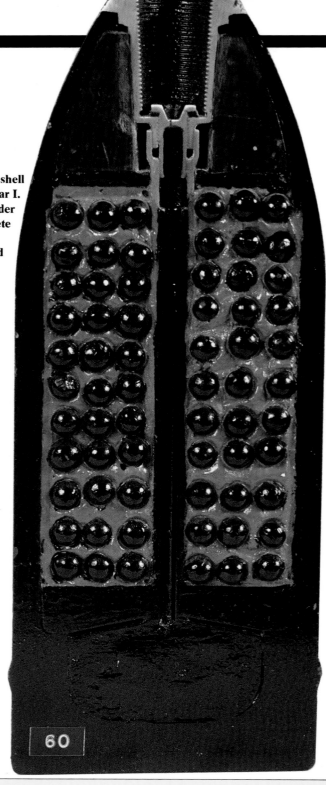

iron mould, with a normal sand mould for the rest of the body. Giving a rapid chill to the nose made the point of the shell extremely hard, and it proved to be a most efficient projectile, one that was rapidly adopted for the RML guns. It is on record that in 1879, during the short war between Chile and Peru, the Chilean *Almirante Cochrane* fired a 9-inch Palliser shell which penetrated the gun turret of the Peruvian *Huascar*, going through 12 centimetres (5.5 inches) of iron plate, 32 centimetres (13 inches) of teak and a further centimetre (half an inch) of steel to explode inside the turret, kill most of the crew, and completely destroy the gun.

For those targets of lesser thickness the 'common shell' was devised; the word 'common' in this case indicates its application to 'common' targets (ie, anything other than thick armour). The common shell was pointed, like a piercing shell, but of plain steel or wrought iron, and was filled with a cotton bag containing coarse gunpowder. After the filling, the bottom of the shell was closed with a simple plug. When the shell struck the target, the sudden check to its flight caused the gunpowder to be thrown violently forward, and friction between the individual grains of powder was sufficient to cause it to explode and burst the shell. It was true that when the shell was fired there was a certain liability for the filling to set back violently, but careful insertion of the powder bag, making sure it was safely lodged at the rear end of the cavity, generally took care that the shell did not explode prematurely.

The greatest problem was adapting the shrapnel shell to the new rifling guns.

Right: A sectioned 18-pounder shrapnel shell dating from World War I. **Centre:** The 18-pounder shrapnel shell complete with fuse. **Far right:** A sectioned 64-pounder shrapnel shell dating from the 1870s.

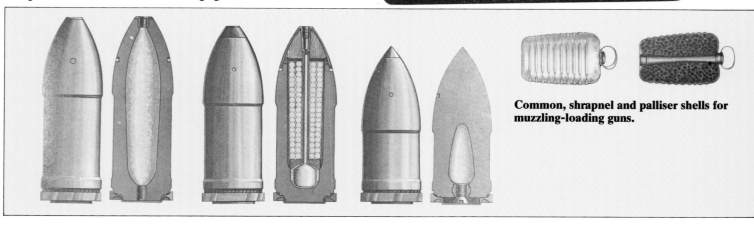

Common, shrapnel and palliser shells for muzzling-loading guns.

Eventually, Colonel Boxer, Superintendent of the Royal Laboratory at Woolwich Arsenal (which was the official ammunition factory) developed a design in which the nose of the shell was lightly pinned to the body and held a socket for a fuze. Beneath the fuze a tube ran down to a chamber in the base of the shell which was filled with gunpowder. Above this chamber was a loose round plate, the 'pusher plate', and above this, taking up the space in the body of the shell around the central tube, was the filling of musket balls packed in resin and coal dust. The shell was fired and the fuze lit, a flash being sent down the central tube to explode the chamber of powder after the fuze had burned through. This explosion forced the pusher plate up, carrying the balls with it, and in turn this force sheared the pins and threw the head of the shell off the body. That then fell to one side and the force of the gunpowder blast ejected all the musket balls in a spreading cone in front of the shell, following the trajectory which the shell was taking. So that if the fuze were correctly set, the shell could be burst in the air some 13 metres (40 feet) above and before the enemy and could then blast him with several score (or hundred, depending upon the size of the shell) musket balls at high velocity. As a man-killer, shrapnel was unrivalled.

Below left: Three wooden time fuzes dating from the mid 19th century.

Below: A diagram showing the construction of a Boxer time fuse.

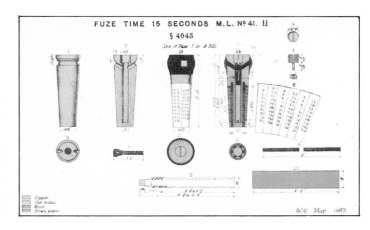

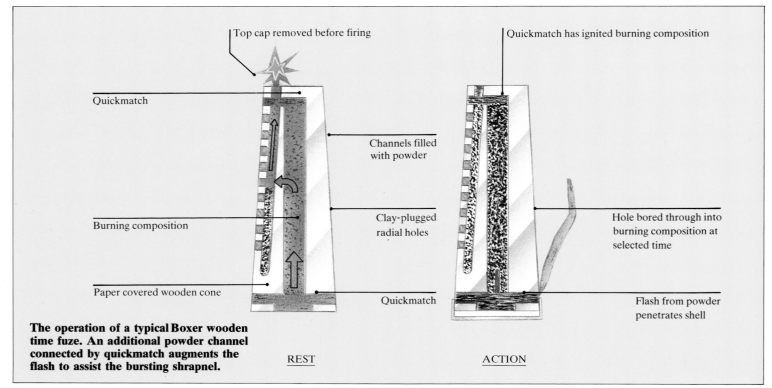

Top cap removed before firing

Quickmatch

Burning composition

Paper covered wooden cone

Channels filled with powder

Clay-plugged radial holes

Quickmatch

Quickmatch has ignited burning composition

Hole bored through into burning composition at selected time

Flash from powder penetrates shell

REST

ACTION

The operation of a typical Boxer wooden time fuze. An additional powder channel connected by quickmatch augments the flash to assist the bursting shrapnel.

It will be appreciated that with a shell as efficient as this, and with guns improving in their range and power, the old-style fuze (which had to be cut to set a time of burning) was somewhat inefficient. Boxer therefore designed a new pattern; it resembled the old insofar as it was a tapering plug of beech wood, but it had some considerable improvements. The central hole was bored in from the top, stopped before reaching the bottom, and was filled with slow-burning powder; above it was a length of quickmatch, coiled up in a recess in the top of the fuze. Parallel with the central hole, and off to the sides of the fuze, another six holes were bored in from the bottom, not reaching the top. More holes were bored in from the sides to connect with these six channels, and the whole system was then filled with gunpowder and the fuze covered in varnished paper. The location of the holes in the sides was indicated by spots of ink, and each hole was given a figure corresponding to the length of powder at that point in the system, each one-tenth of an inch being worth half a second of flight.

The fuze was 'bored' by a gimlet prior to firing. The desired time having been

selected, the gimlet was forced into the hole corresponding to the required length, and bored through the interior wood until it entered the central channel. The fuze was then put in the shell and the shell fired. The flash-over around the shell ignited the quickmatch in the head; this lit the slow-burning composition in the central hole; in turn this burned steadily until it came to the point to which the gimlet had been bored in, whereupon the flame passed through the hole and ignited the gunpowder in one of the outer channels. The gunpowder immediately flashed down its length to the bottom of the fuze and ignited the contents of the shell.

The flash-over which lit the fuze was a mixed blessing. Whereas it was useful in that respect, it caused problems in the gun itself, washing away the steel of the bore as it forced its way past the shell and wasting energy which should have been applied behind the shell to give it more velocity. After experiments with rope wads and other ineffective methods, a 'gas-check' was devised in the form of a saucer-shaped copper plate bolted to the bottom of the shell. Its diameter was slightly less than that of the shell body, so that on being rammed

down the muzzle it passed within the rifling. When the charge exploded behind it, the soft copper was forced outwards by the gases and bit into the rifling, sealing off the escape of gas and allowing all the gas to be devoted to propelling the shell. This considerably improved the wear and tear on the gun — but it now failed to ignite the fuze, and so Boxer had to re-design his fuze by putting a small firing pin and cap in the nose. As the shell was suddenly accelerated, so the firing pin was forced back to hit the cap and this ignited the central powder channel.

The most acceptable thing about the rifled gun, so far as ammunition designers were concerned, was that the shell now arrived point-first with regularity. This meant that for the first time it became possible to fit a percussion, or impact, fuze which would operate when the shell struck the target. There was nothing complex about the design: it was merely the usual sort of plug with a firing pin and cap, so that on impact the pin was driven into the cap to fire a small charge of powder which, in turn, flashed back into the shell. The shells used with this type of fuze were for anti-personnel effect in the field and either

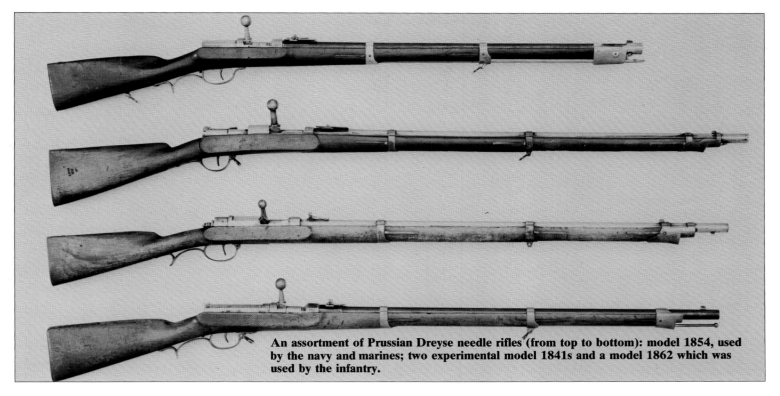

An assortment of Prussian Dreyse needle rifles (from top to bottom): model 1854, used by the navy and marines; two experimental model 1841s and a model 1862 which was used by the infantry.

relied upon the shattering of the wrought-iron casing by the gunpowder inside or, in a few cases, used artificial methods of producing the requisite fragments. One common pattern was the 'ring shell' in which the body was built up of a series of segments of iron encased in lead or zinc, so that when the central bursting charge exploded the segments were blasted separately in all directions as they burst the outer casing.

At this point the artillerymen may be seen to have regained the position they had earlier lost to the infantry, and we may go back to see what had been happening in the small-arms world.

Breech-loading had, in fact, made an impact on small arms earlier than it had on artillery. The German gunsmith von Dreyse invented the 'Needle Gun' in 1838, basing his invention on an idea first put

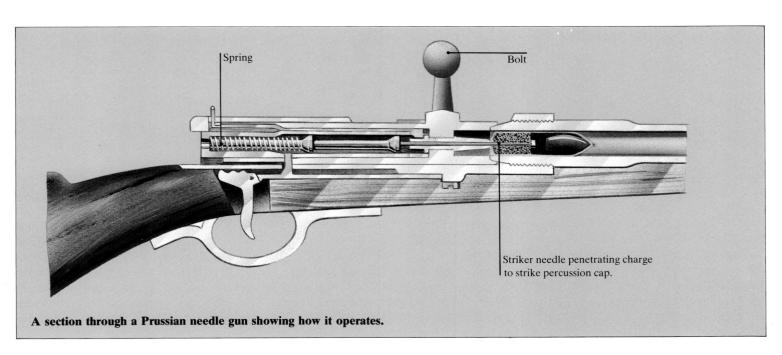

Spring

Bolt

Striker needle penetrating charge to strike percussion cap.

A section through a Prussian needle gun showing how it operates.

forward by Pauly, a Frenchman, some years before. In brief, the rear of the gun was closed by a bolt which worked like a common door-bolt; when thrust forward it forced its tapered end into the rear of the gun chamber, and the handle, turned down in front of a lug on the gun body, prevented the explosion blowing the bolt open. A long spring-propelled needle ran down the centre of the bolt. The Dreyse cartridge consisted of a paper package comprising a conoidal bullet with a percussion cap in its base, and a paper cylinder of gunpowder. This was placed in the chamber and the bolt closed. When the trigger was pulled the needle flew forward and pierced all the way through the cartridge until it struck the cap and fired it. This ignited the powder charge and the bullet was propelled up the rifled barrel. The bolt was then re-opened, the firing pin cocked, a new cartridge inserted, and the gun was ready to fire again, far faster than a muzzle-loader could be prepared.

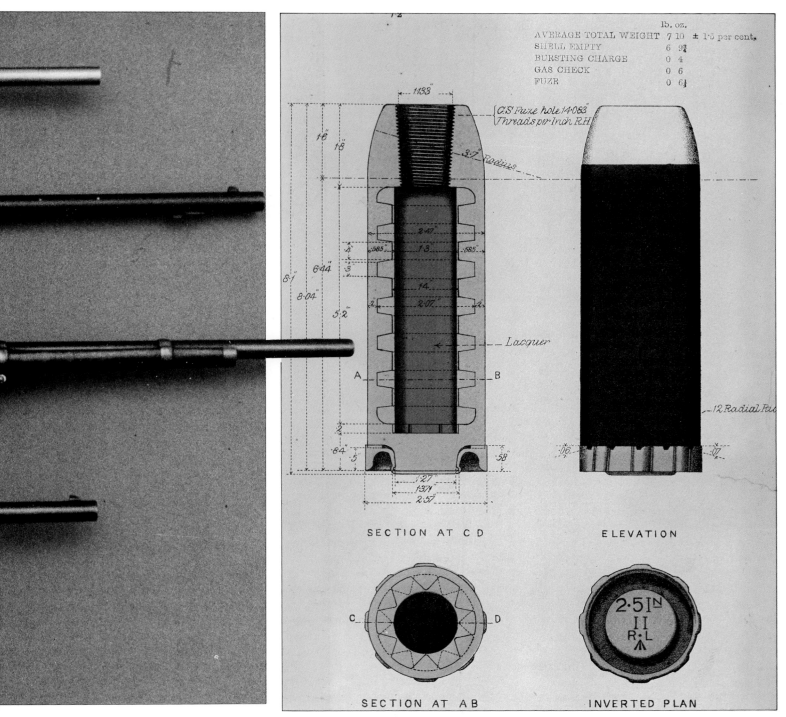

	lb.	oz.
AVERAGE TOTAL WEIGHT	7	10 ± 1·5 per cent.
SHELL EMPTY	6	9¾
BURSTING CHARGE	0	4
GAS CHECK	0	6
FUZE	0	6¼

SECTION AT C D   ELEVATION

SECTION AT A B   INVERTED PLAN

Above: A selection of American Sharps carbines. The paper cartridge was sliced open by the closing breech block.

Above right: A 2.5in ring shell which would be muzzle loaded. The ridges around the base would engage the rifling inside the barrel.

The French Army, ever fearful of what the Germans might be up to, were alarmed at the thought of this advanced weapon on the other side of their frontier and set about developing something similar: the 'Chassepot', named after its inventor. The Chassepot also used a bolt system, and the bolt carried a thick rubber sealing ring at its front end. The cartridge was similar to that of the Needle Gun, except that the cap was at the back end of the cartridge so the firing pin did not need to pass entirely through the cartridge. Both of these weapons had their drawbacks, but for their time they were efficient and formidable. The performance of both guns aroused a good

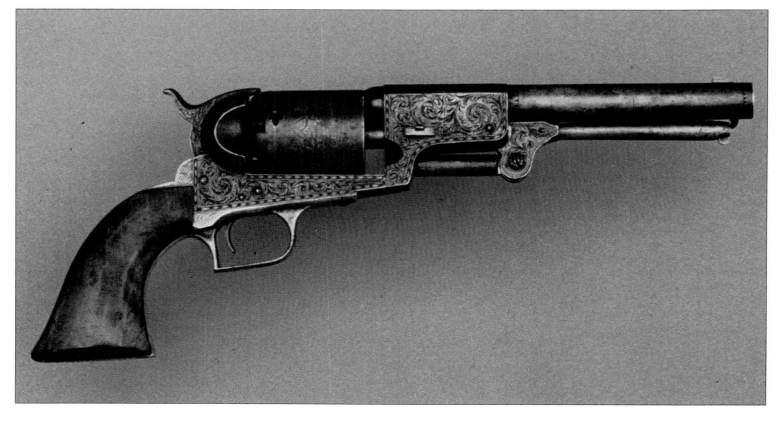

The Colt revolver. It owed its pre-eminence to Samuel Colt's master patent on the revolving cylinder.

deal of interest when France and Germany met in the war of 1870.

The American Sharps carbine showed a different approach to breech closure, using a metal block that was lifted and lowered by a lever underneath the butt. A self-contained paper cartridge was again used, which was loaded into the chamber and the breech closed; as the breech block came up so it sliced off the rear end of the paper cartridge, leaving the powder loosely exposed inside the chamber. A percussion cap was then placed on a nipple and hammer-fired (in other words, the Sharps cartridge did not have self-contained ignition as did the Dreyse and Chassepot designs).

Another interesting idea from about this period (the 1850s) was the Volcanic rifle, developed by — among others — two Americans called Smith and Wesson who were to go on to greater fame. The Volcanic used a bullet that had a hollow rear section filled with powder and closed by a cardboard wad with a central hole; it

was inserted into the breech and the breech block raised to close. A cap was placed on a nipple on the breech and hammer-fired. The flash passed through the hole in the wad, ignited the powder, and the explosion blew the bullet from the gun. The idea was sound, but the breech sealing was practically non-existent, and the quantity of powder in the bullet was so small that the Volcanics could not achieve much velocity. After about six years of endeavour to solve the problem, Smith & Wesson gave up the struggle and turned their attention to a more promising project.

What they turned to was a revolver. At that time Samuel Colt had the revolver business thoroughly sewn up, thanks to a master patent covering mechanical methods of rotating the revolver cylinder. But the patent was due to expire in 1857, and Smith & Wesson intended to step in with a new design. Casting about for some novelty, they chanced on a new device that had been invented in France — the metallic rimfire cartridge.

The idea of putting everything — bullet, charge and cap — into a single unit had, as is demonstrated by the existence of the Needle Gun, attracted many experiments, but the failure rate was high, largely because of the problems involved in sealing the breech. Eventually, in 1836, a French gunmaker called Lefaucheaux devised a weapon in which the barrel was hinged and could be 'broken' away from the breech — the pattern which is today familiar in shotguns. He made use of a self-contained cartridge, designed by a man called Houiller, in which most of the case was of paper but with a short brass cap at the rear end, the bullet at the front, and the powder charge inside the paper section. Inside the brass end-piece was a percussion cap, with a short pin above it, aligned so as to protrude through the side of the brass section. The cartridge was loaded into the breech, the pin passing down a slot in the end of the barrel as the gun was closed. The pin now stood proud of the barrel where it could be struck by a hammer; striking fired the cap, the charge exploded and expelled the bullet, and the brass section was expanded tightly against the walls of the chambers by the explosion, so sealing the breech against any escape of gas to the rear.

The 'pin-fire' cartridge revolutionized gun design and shooting overnight — but another design that was already being drawn up would eventually replace it. Another Frenchman, Flobert, took the percussion cap, removed the rim from the front and inserted a tiny lead bullet. He then adapted the Lefaucheaux gun and made the hammer strike a short pin which, in turn, struck the percussion cap to fire the bullet. Such a weapon was obviously small and weak, but it proved popular for indoor shooting at targets. Flobert then improved the idea by changing the shape of the cap slightly, giving it a protruding rim which butted against the rear of the barrel and kept the loaded cartridge in the proper place. The rim was folded and hollow, and filled with percussion mixture. Flobert filled the rest of the tube with powder and placed a bullet in the fore end. His rifle was so designed that the hammer struck against the rim of the cartridge, crushing the composition inside against the edge of the barrel and so igniting the powder. The rimfire cartridge was born.

Smith and Wesson now adopted this rimfire for their revolver. The cartridge required a cylinder with holes bored all the way through, so that it could be loaded from the rear. When Smith & Wesson discovered that a patent existed for this arrangement, they bought up the patent and by so doing put themselves in a position to control revolver manufacture as soon as Colt's patent expired.

The success of the Smith & Wesson revolver with the rimfire cartridge stimulated interest, and many alternative designs of rimfire appeared, particularly in the United States of America, during the following years.

But the rimfire, as it was built in those days, had one defect — it tended to be relatively low-powered. If the rim was to be crushed, the case metal had to be fairly soft, and this argued against high-powered cartridges, since they might well blow out through the soft rim.

Above: A cased Smith and Wesson revolver. They exploited the expiry of Colt's patent in 1857 with the introduction of the metallic rimfire cartridge in the US. This had been invented in France by a man named Houiller, while the breaking action had been devised by Lefaucheaux.

Right: A selection of early small arms cartridges, including a dumdum-style bullet with a flat head and an explosive shell.

The next move was to take the existing percussion cap and the metallic cartridge and marry the two together, placing the cap in the centre of the case base and striking it with a hammer or a firing pin. There were several separate attempts at this before the final successful designs appeared, but by about 1875 the centre-fire metallic cartridge was in being and fast becoming the standard method of charging a hand or shoulder firearm. It became possible to make cartridges of any desired power in the centre-fire pattern, because the cap was

supported from behind by the breech closing system.

By the late 1870s the breech-loading hand arm was appearing in all sorts of guises and with all sorts of mechanisms, and the artillery designers began to take a second look at the possibility of breech-loading for cannon. Engineering had made some advances since Armstrong's day and there now seemed to be a possibility to make gun breeches of sufficient strength to withstand heavy charges. Two systems appeared to hold particular promise: the

first was the sliding block breech developed by Krupp of Germany, and the second was the interrupted screw breech which appeared in France.

The Krupp system resembled the Armstrong insofar as the gun ended in an open-sided box; but instead of Armstrong's 'vent piece' the Krupp gun used a slab of steel which slid sideways to close the chamber. After experimenting with various ideas for sealing the breech against the escape of gas, Krupp adopted the metallic cartridge case which had proved so successful in small

The breech of a French gun, circa 1800, showing the de Bange breech screw. The breech is opened by rotating the handle to the vertical to unlock the thread.

Left: The shell and cartridge case — standing upright behind — for Krupp's largest gun, the 80cm railway gun.

Below: A drawing from 1870 showing the Krupp coastal defence gun. A crane was needed to load the ammunition.

arms. Despite later development, he never changed from this system in subsequent years, even for his largest gun, the 80cm (31.5-inch) calibre railway gun of World War II, a monster which fired a 7,100kg (7-ton) shell. The metal cartridge case for this weapon was 1.3m long and 96cm in diameter, and carried a charge weighing 2,240kg (just over two tons).

The interrupted screw breech constituted a more difficult engineering problem (which is one reason Krupp stayed clear of it once he had a working system). The rear end of the gun had an enlarged diameter behind the chamber which was cut with a very coarse screw-thread; this then had longitudinal segments of the thread milled away. The breech block was a cylinder which was made with a matching screw-thread and then, again, had sections milled away, so that both chamber and block had three plain and three threaded sections along their lengths. If the block were now aligned so that the threaded sections slid into the plain sections in the chamber, the block could be inserted into the gun. Once inserted to its full depth, close against the end of the chamber, it could be given a one-third turn so as to bring all the threaded sections into engagement. This would then resist any pressure that might tend to thrust the block out again.

The problem now lay with sealing the breech block and chamber joint. The earliest guns did it by fitting a short steel cup on the front of the block; this entered the chamber behind the cartridge and was expanded tightly against the chamber walls by the explosion, in just the same manner as

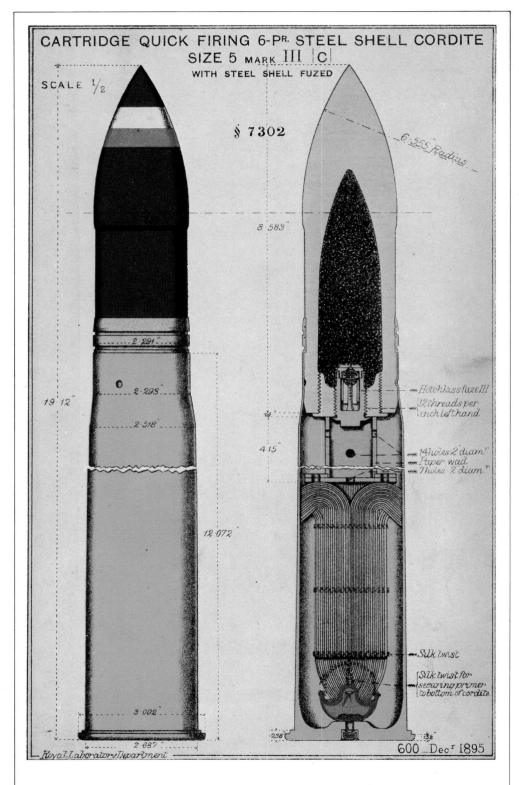

CARTRIDGE QUICK FIRING 6-PR. STEEL SHELL CORDITE
SIZE 5 MARK III C
WITH STEEL SHELL FUZED

SCALE ½

§ 7302

A fixed round of heavy ammunition — a quick-firing 6-pounder shell, sectioned to show its construction.

Above: A contemporary drawing of a battery of French 75mm quick-firing guns at practice. Fixed rounds considerably speeded the process of reloading.

Right: A fixed round of shrapnel for the 13-pounder horse artillery gun widely used in World War I.

a cartridge case was expanded inside a small arm. However, experience soon showed that the steel cup not only soon began to erode from the hot gases but was often battered and bent as the breech block was opened and closed. A better idea came from another French designer, de Bangé, who fitted a resilient pad of asbestos and oil to the front end of the block and then secured it in place with a 'mushroom head' of steel. The stem of the mushroom passed through the breech block and was secured by a nut at the rear; it also had a vent bored through to accommodate the ignition flame. The sealing pad was trapped beneath the mushroom head, and when the gun fired the pressure pushed back on the head and squeezed the pad outwards to seal against the side of the chamber. Even

without going into abstruse mathematics it can be shown that the outward pressure on the pad is always in excess of whatever the interior pressure inside the gun may be, so that sealing is always assured. The de Bangé system, with periodic refinements, has been used ever since on major-calibre artillery.

The next step in artillery ammunition was to marry the shell and cartridge together into a single unit, as was common in small arms ammunition. This would allow a gun to be loaded much more quickly by simply inserting the complete one-piece round, instead of loading the shell, ramming it, then loading the cartridge behind it. The first guns to adopt a method using 'fixed ammunition' were three- and six-pounder guns (1.85- and

2.224-inch calibre) for naval use. These became known as 'quick-firers' because the speed of loading allowed a very high rate of fire to be achieved, up to perhaps 20 shots per minute with a skilled crew. It was also made possible by the fact that each gun was anchored securely on a steel mount to a steel deck on a warship, so that the force of recoil was absorbed by the ship's structure.

When the same principle was attempted in a field-gun, problems arose: such a high rate of fire was impossible because the gun on firing rolled back under the force of recoil and the gunners had to get it back into place and re-lay before another shot could be fired.

The French Army solved this problem with their famous 75mm gun of 1897. It used a hydraulic cylinder beneath the barrel which carried a piston rod connected to the gun in such a way that at the recoil it was dragged through the cylinder, its movement resisted by oil. As it displaced oil, so it built up pressure in a compartment of nitrogen gas, which also acted to brake the movement of the gun. Once the gun's recoil stopped, the gas pressure forced the piston head back inside the cylinder and pulled the gun barrel back into the firing position. The gun carriage remained stationary — only the barrel moved — and the gunners could thus remain clustered around the breech. A fixed round of ammunition was used and the '75' could achieve 20 shots a minute with ease. It became the pattern for the field-guns of the 20th century.

During the time that breech-loading was making its return, rifling was also being improved. The universal method now evolved was to cut a large number of spiral grooves into the bore of the gun and fit the shell with a 'driving band' or 'rotating band' of soft copper. This was sunk into the steel wall of the shell and anchored securely; as the shell entered the bore of the gun the copper bit into the rifling and the shell took up spin.

During the last 20 years of the 19th century a major revolution in ammunition technology took place when gunpowder was at last toppled from its monopoly position as the universal explosive. As a propelling charge gunpowder had its faults. It was susceptible to damp, and deposited dirt and fouling in the gun barrel, necessitating frequent cleaning. It also gave out a cloud of white smoke when it fired, which immediately gave away the position of the weapon and, when hundreds of weapons were in use, contributed to covering the battlefield in an impenetrable 'fog of war' which made command and control virtually impossible. As a bursting charge for putting inside a shell it was, again, prone to damp, gave off white smoke when it burst (which was acceptable since it at least showed where the shell had landed), broke the shell up into a few large fragments, and was always liable to premature explosion due to friction if the filling had been carried out carelessly.

Throughout the 19th century there had

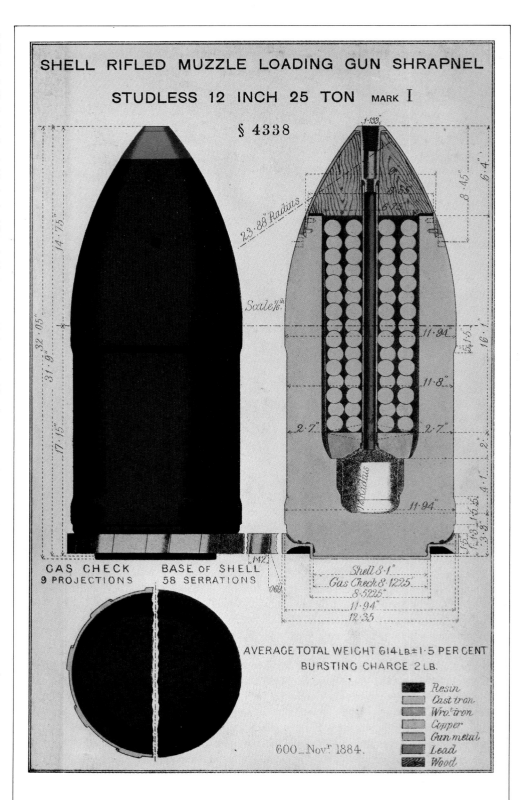

A shrapnel shell for the British 12in rifled muzzle-loading coastal gun. This ammunition provided an effective defence against landing parties.

been innumerable advances in chemistry. In 1846 Schönbein had discovered 'gun-cotton', made by the action of nitric and sulphuric acids on cotton. It was a devastating explosive, although it proved difficult to manufacture (several factories were blown to pieces before the process was mastered). It eventually found use as a demolition explosive and as a filling for mines and torpedoes — but as a propellant it was entirely useless: the principal difficulty was that when ignited gun-cotton would detonate, rather than explode. An explosion is a rapid burning process and is, to some degree, capable of being controlled; a detonation is the molecular disruption of a substance — much faster and more violent than an explosion, and quite uncontrollable. So making a propelling charge of gun-cotton simply blew the gun to pieces as it detonated.

Nitroglycerine was discovered in 1846, but it was not until the 1870s that Nobel managed to produce it in quantity without blowing up the factory and, again, it was so violent and sensitive that nobody could see any application for it in ammunition.

The first successful substitute for gun-powder was discovered by Major Schultze of the Prussian Artillery in 1865; it was made of nitrated wood impregnated with potassium salts. It was followed by 'EC Powder', made in England by The Explosives Company, which was nitrated cotton impregnated with potassium nitrate. These powders exploded, and they were widely adopted for sporting use in shotguns, but they proved to be too violent for rifled weapons, and it was not until 1886 that Vielle in France developed the first 'smokeless powder' which could be used in a military rifle. The French Army had selected a small-calibre rifle, the 8mm Lebel, as their future weapon and the Vieille powder — named *Poudre B* after General Boulanger — became the standard propellant.

The British 'War Department Chemist', Professor Abel, spent several years working on various compounds before he perfected Cordite in 1889. This was a mixture of nitroglycerine and nitro cellulose made in the form of cords or sticks (and hence its name); because it was possible to make it in

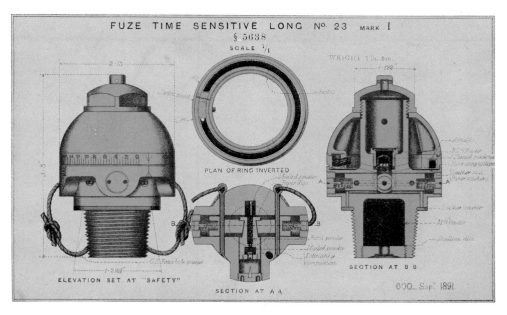

A metal time fuze — the length of fuze is adjusted by turning the top.

any desired size it rapidly became the standard military propellant for both small arms and artillery.

Compared with gunpowder, smokeless powders had great advantages: they were virtually smokeless, they were much less susceptible to damp, they would last longer in store and, weight for weight, they were much more powerful. Moreover, the size and shape of the individual sticks or grains could be made exactly as required so that the burning rate could be controlled to give the desired ballistics. Against all this was the drawback that the flame temperature of these powders was much higher than that of gunpowder, and they therefore had a severely erosive effect on the interior of the gun barrel. A weapon which might fire 10,000 shots with gunpowder could well be worn out after 5,000 with smokeless.

By 1914 the general design of ammunition had reached a fairly uniform standard throughout the world. Revolvers used brass-cased cartridges with lead bullets. The few automatic pistols used similar cartridges but usually with bullets having a lead core and a covering of copper, because they were usually higher-velocity weapons and a lead bullet tended to leave a deposit in the barrel when fired at these velocities. Rifle ammunition was similarly brass-

cased, using a bullet with lead core and copper or steel jacket. Artillery ammunition used either a brass case to contain the charge, or a silk bag, depending upon whether the gun used a sliding block breech or an interrupted screw system. Shells were either 'common', 'piercing' or 'shrapnel'.

The common shell was still filled with gunpowder, although some armies had developed more violent fillings — the British used 'Lyddite', which was their name for solid picric acid, and many other countries used it also under different names. The Germans were beginning to use TNT (tri-nitro-toluene) which was more powerful than picric acid but was much more difficult to detonate.

Piercing shells were by now made of specially hardened steel, and had a very small filling of explosive in the base, together with a delayed-action fuze which caused the explosive to detonate after the shell had pierced the armour of the target.

To make the shrapnel shell work, the time fuze was no longer a bored-out piece of wood but a complex metal device which screwed into the head of the shell. Usually of brass, it consisted of a core containing a firing pin and cap which ignited a train of gunpowder set into a brass ring surrounding the core. Beneath this ring the body of

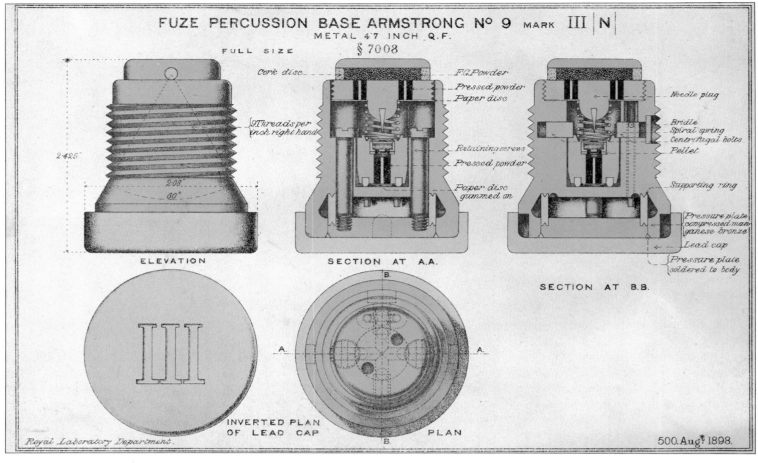

Armstrong percussion base fuze.

the fuze carried another, similar, train of powder which led to a small compartment at the bottom of the fuze, also powder-filled. Before loading, the fuze was set to the desired time by turning the lower, moveable, ring until an arrow was correctly adjusted against an engraved scale. On firing, the pin hit the cap, giving a flash which ignited the powder in the top ring at the specified point along the train. This burned, at a carefully regulated speed, until it came to the end of the train whereupon it flashed down through a hole in the bottom of the ring and lit the train in the fuze body. This, in turn, burned until it ignited the charge of powder which then made the shell function. Turning the loose ring varied the length of the powder train which had to burn before the various transfers of flame took place, and so regulated the operating time of the fuze.

World War I brought several new items

into the ammunition world because new targets made their appearance and new tactical ideas demanded specialized ammunition to make them work. One of the first innovations was the hand-grenade. Although a grenade had been seen in the past, it had generally been a small cast-iron mortar shell with a simple length of slow match fuze; the fuze was lit and the shell tossed (for example) over the ramparts of a fort to upset any attacking parties in the ditch. When that sort of warfare faded, so did the use of the grenade, and it was not until the Russo-Japanese War of 1904 that it reappeared in small numbers. This led to some research on the idea, so that when grenades were demanded in 1914 for trench warfare, there were a few designs in existence and more were soon developed. As is often the case, it took time to get these designs into production and for the first few months the soldiers were filling jam tins

and empty containers of all sorts with gunpowder and stones, fitting a short length of fuze, and throwing them at the enemy.

The rifle-grenade was developed for those occasions when the hand-grenade was wanted but for long distances. In the first designs the projecting was done by fitting the grenade with a long thin rod which was inserted into the barrel of a rifle; a blank cartridge (one without a bullet) was inserted into the breech, the weapon elevated to about 45°, and the cartridge fired. This blew the rod and grenade out, the rod acted as a stabilizing tail, and the grenade would go to 100 or 150 metres range. Unfortunately, the sudden check to the gas pressure as it endeavoured to lift almost one kilogram (2lb) of grenade out of the barrel often caused local bulging of the barrel, and rifles used for firing rod-grenades were soon useless.

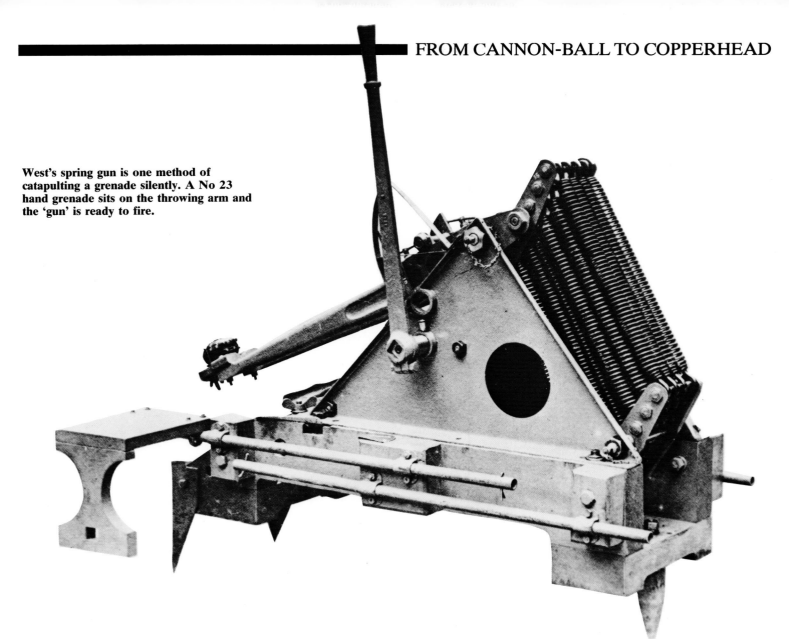

West's spring gun is one method of catapulting a grenade silently. A No 23 hand grenade sits on the throwing arm and the 'gun' is ready to fire.

The next move was to clamp a cup on the muzzle of the rifle and put the grenade inside, with a round plate behind it to act as a gas check. The blank cartridge now developed sufficient gas to fill the cup and blow the grenade out without doing any damage to the rifle barrel, so it could still be used to shoot bullets. But the strain on the weapon of firing heavy grenades often loosened the woodwork and made the rifle inaccurate.

Next came the trench mortar, a short-barrelled gun for pitching shells into the air and dropping them into the opposing trenches. The German Army had a design ready when the war began, but it was an expensive and complicated breech-loading weapon. After several home-made designs had been tried, an English engineer called William Stokes came forward with a design he had perfected in his own factory. It was the essence of simplicity: a smooth-bored tube, closed at the rear end and with a fixed firing pin, supported on a baseplate and a simple two-legged stand. The 'bomb' was a

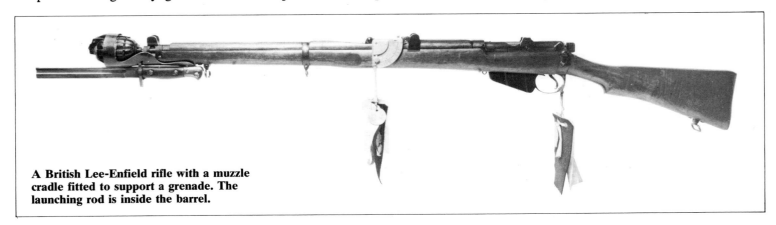

A British Lee-Enfield rifle with a muzzle cradle fitted to support a grenade. The launching rod is inside the barrel.

cylinder of cast iron with a modified hand-grenade fuze on the front end and with a perforated tube carrying a shotgun cartridge full of smokeless powder at the rear end. When this was dropped down the tube the shotgun cartridge cap struck the fixed firing pin, and the subsequent explosion lifted the bomb out of the tube and propelled it for about 700 metres on a high trajectory so that it dropped almost vertically into the enemy trench.

The development of aircraft for warfare set off a demand for guns for air defence, which posed considerable problems. A normal shrapnel or explosive shell could deal with aircraft if the gunner could get it close enough, but the major problem was that he had little or no idea where his shell

had gone in relation to the target. The first requirement was to mark the flight of the shell so that corrections could be made — and this led to the development of the tracer shell.

The first types used a liquid, carried in a compartment below the main explosive filling of the shell; this had a small port leading to the outside, plugged with solder. As the shell was fired, the friction as it went up the bore melted the solder and as the shell spun through the air the black liquid was thrown out through the port by centrifugal force, leaving a dark line in the air behind it. As might be imagined, this was a good enough system in broad daylight but of limited value when the light was poor, and it was soon replaced by pyrotechnic

tracers. These used magnesium compounds pressed into a tube screwed into the base of the shell. The flash from the charge lit the magnesium and this burned as the shell went through the air, giving the impression of a streak of light marking out the trajectory.

The next problem was that if the shell missed the target — as most of them did — it was liable to fall back to earth and then go off, to the discomfort of anyone it happened to land on. Understandably, impact fuzes had to be abandoned and only time fuzes used, so that even if the shell missed it would detonate in the sky at the end of the set time. Fragments would indeed still rain down on the people beneath, but they were less liable to do harm than a primed and

Above: A group of German staff officers inspect captured equipment, including a British 9.45in trench mortar.

Above left: These aerial torpedoes — so called because of their long tail-fins — were fired out of trench mortars and delivered a large charge at close range.

Right: An early British mortar, the Vickers 1.75in 'toffee apple'. The round bomb has a stick tail inside the mortar barrel.

filled shell. The discovery then followed that time fuzes fired into the upper reaches of the atmosphere performed differently from those fired at ground-level targets, and it took the better part of three years' hard work and testing before all the problems were solved.

One thing that caught all contemporary belligerents unawares was the immense appetite for ammunition that modern warfare was consumed by. The replacement programme for field-gun shells for the French Army, for example, called for the manufacture of 3,600 shells per day; this may sound a lot — but the French had 1,200 guns in the front line, so the programme really meant three shots per gun per day. Factories had to be built to manufacture the shells and the explosives, the fuzes and the cartridges, and assembly plants had to fit them all together . . . and it all took a year or more to reach the point at which the supply could keep up with the demand. The German Army were caught as badly as anyone else, and even before the end of 1914 they were looking for some substitute for explosive which they could put into shells. The answer was to use gas.

It is often said that the Germans first used gas against the British at Ypres, Belgium, in April 1915, but this is not true; the first use of gas was in shells fired against the Russians on the Eastern Front in January 1915. These shells were filled with xylyl bromide, a tear gas, but because of a slight oversight on the part of the Germans they failed to have any effect. What they had overlooked was the severity of the Russian winter: the gas froze solid and failed to disperse. The next use, chlorine gas released from cylinders against the British at Ypres, was far more effective, which is why it is often regarded as the first application of the gas weapon.

Left: The King examines a gas bomb at the Gun School Helfaut, 7 July 1917. Below: Section view of captured German gas shells. Right: Loading a smoothbore 18cm German projector. Far right: Phosphorus bullets being used to shoot down a Zeppelin during World War I.

But from this beginning the gas war proliferated. All three contesting armies used gas shells fired from a variety of guns and howitzers. Trench mortars were also used since they were able to carry a greater percentage of gas in their bombs. The most effective device was the British 'Livens Projector', a wide-barrelled mortar which pitched a drum containing 13.6kg (30lbs) of gas into the enemy trenches. These projectors were strung out in long ranks behind the British trenches and fired simultaneously so as to deliver the maximum amount of gas in the shortest possible time. They proved to be extremely effective.

Small-arms ammunition also developed in response to particular problems. Again, the first demand was for a bullet that would allow machine-gunners to fire at aircraft, and this led to the development of tracer bullets. The principal aerial target in the early part of World War I was the Zeppelin airship, and demand rose for an incendiary bullet capable of igniting the hydrogen gas that kept the Zeppelin airborne. This development was closely linked with the tracer development — since one bullet, properly designed, could do both jobs — although some specialized incendiary bullets appeared. The small size of rifle and machine-gun bullets ruled out the use of complicated fuzes or fillings, and the eventual result was a hollow bullet filled with phosphorus and with one or two holes drilled into it. These holes were plugged with solder and, as with the early tracer shell, friction in the bore melted the solder and spin caused the phosphorus to trickle out of the bullet in flight. Phosphorus has the useful property of being self-igniting when exposed to the air, so there was no requirement for caps for ignition systems. The burning material itself would ignite the hydrogen as it pierced the gas-bags.

When the first tanks arrived on the battlefield there was a demand for bullets which would penetrate the armour. The answer came in the form of a bullet which carried a hard steel core inside the conventional copper jacket, so that when it struck, the core passed through the copper and penetrated the armour plate.

Phosphorus was also used on the ground to provide smoke so that an obscuring cloud could be laid on the ground to conceal the movement of troops behind it. All that was necessary was to put sufficient explosive into the shell to crack it open and allow the phosphorus to reach the air, whereupon it caught fire and produced a dense white smoke. It was also found that the flying phosphorus made an excellent incendiary material when it landed on buildings or equipment, and it turned out additionally to be an extremely painful substance when it landed on the body. The biggest drawback was that phosphorus-filled ammunition had to be very carefully manufactured so that it did not leak in storage — more than one ammunition dump was destroyed by a fire begun by a leaking smoke-shell.

The star shell was perfected in order to see what the enemy was up to at night. It had existed in one form or another for many years, usually as a simple shell which blew open and ejected one or two firework stars which lay on the ground and burned. But a better result was obtained by bursting the shell in the air and suspending the star from a parachute, so that it floated slowly down and illuminated a large area beneath it as it did so.

At the end of the war, in 1918, ammunition development virtually stopped. The survivors had, after all, lived through 'the war to end wars', so there was a general slackening of all military development, and the principal activity was to take the wartime designs, many of which had been hurriedly put together, and consider refinements and improvements. One of a few significant developments of the period was the British invention of a new type of smoke-shell. The white phosphorus shell was simple to make but had the technical drawback that the heat of burning warmed up the air around the smoke; the hot air

Above: White phosphorus smoke shells contain enough explosive to crack on impact, exposing the phosphorus to the air.

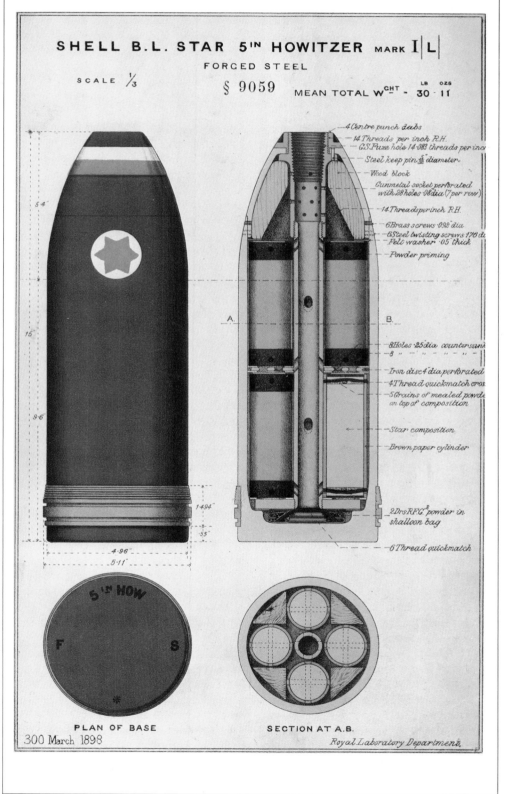

Right: The construction of an early version of the star shell which did not have a parachute to slow its descent.

rose and took the smoke with it, so that instead of a low-lying cloud to obscure the view, there was a series of pillars of smoke with frequent gaps. The new idea was the 'base ejection' shell in which the smoke composition, based on hexachlorethane and powdered zinc, was packed into canisters each of which had a perforated tube running through its centre. Three or four of these canisters could be packed into a shell body, topped by a pusher plate and a charge of gunpowder, and the base of the shell was screwed or pinned into place. A time fuze at the nose ignited the gunpowder expelling charge at the proper time, the charge exploded, and the flash passed down the central tubes of the canisters and lit the smoke composition. The pressure due to the explosion then forced down on the canisters, burst open the base of the shell and allowed the canisters to fall to the ground where they continued to emit smoke. The empty shell went on to fall harmlessly, while the smoke developed by the mixture was cool and stuck close to the ground to make a thick and continuous screen.

The other major change was the final abandonment of the shrapnel shell. Shrapnel was at its best against masses of troops advancing in the open, but the 1914-18 war had been conducted largely in trenches and under cover, and shrapnel had had little effect in these conditions. The high-explosive shell was far more useful, being able to wreck the cover and kill by fragmentation and blast, and so the high-explosive shell became the standard artillery projectile in the 1930s.

There was also a change in the operation of time fuzes. In 1916 the British had picked up fragments of German shrapnel shells which had landed more or less undamaged and had discovered that the fuze contained a clockwork mechanism. It was a fully-wound clock which ran for up to 60 seconds, and at the end of the set time a catch was released which fired a detonator to operate the shell. Work began in Britain on developing a similar fuze, but the difficulties were enormous and it was not until the middle 1920s that a successful design was achieved. Unfortunately the mass-production of such a device

demanded a watch-making industry — which Britain did not have — and so the mechanical time fuze was produced only in very small numbers for demonstration purposes. It was to take the outbreak of another war, and the loosening of the public purse-strings, to get such a device into production.

In the 1930s a number of German officers began to question the form of the infantryman's rifle and its ammunition. The standard type of rifle, which had evolved around the turn of the century, was a weapon firing a powerful cartridge, capable of accurate shooting out to 900 metres (1,000 yards) range and of being used in a machine-gun to as far as 2,700 metres (3,000 yards). But careful examination of soldiers who fought in the war, and study of records, seemed to indicate that few soldiers ever saw an enemy farther away than about 350 metres (400 yards), and very few ever attempted to fire a rifle at ranges over 450 metres (500 yards). It seemed illogical to burden the man with a heavy rifle and a powerful cartridge when he did not need the power they had been designed to deliver. It would be more sensible, said the Germans, to make a cartridge with a shorter case and lighter bullet; this would give less recoil, the rifle could be shorter and lighter, and the man could carry more cartridges.

The reasoning was perfectly sound, but the objection was simply that Germany had several hundreds of millions of cartridges of the regulation size, and changing the rifle and all that ammunition would be prohibitively expensive. And so, although some design work was done on a 'short cartridge', nothing else happened.

When war broke out again in 1939, armies went to war with much the same weapons and ammunition that they had ended with in 1918. Behind the scenes, however, intensive research was in progress which would bear fruit later in the war.

The first area of concern for the soldier in 1939 was how to stop a tank. Most countries had small anti-tank guns — about 37−40mm calibre, firing solid steel shot — and the infantry were generally provided with high-powered rifles firing armour-

piercing bullets, but the way tank design was progressing it was only a matter of time before these would be incapable of dealing with the increased thickness of armour. It seemed that the only way to defeat armour was to throw a very hard projectile at very high speed, so several designers simply made guns with more powerful cartridges. But they then ran up against a new problem: when a steel shot hits a hard target at more than about 800 metres per second (2,600fps) velocity, the shock of impact is so great that the steel shot disintegrates without making much impression. To prevent this, one solution was to protect the tip of the shot with a soft steel cap which, more or less, acted as a 'shock absorber' and allowed the tip of the shot to penetrate. Unfortunately, the best shape for this 'penetrative cap' was not the best flight shape, so a second 'ballistic cap' of thin steel had to be put in front. But these caps merely lifted the 'shatter velocity'

explosive inside a cavity hollowed out in the form of a cone or hemisphere. This cavity was then lined with a thin copper plate of appropriate shape, and the fuze was arranged to detonate the explosive at the end farthest from the cavity and liner. The detonation wave, sweeping forward through the explosive, collapsed the liner, and the cavity shape 'focused' the blast into a very fast moving jet of hot gas and molten metal which punched through steel armour as if it were cardboard. A 75mm shell could easily defeat 100mm of armour plate. Although the hole was small — no more than 1.2 centimetres (half an inch) across — the hot jet passed through into the tank and did immense damage if it struck something vital, such as a fuel tank, ammunition or, of course, a member of the crew.

The hollow-charge principle could also be applied to demolition weapons. Its first use during the war came when German glider-borne troops used such bombs to punch through the armoured turrets of Fort Eben Emael during the attack on Belgium in 1940.

While the hollow charge was being developed, work had gone forward on trying to solve the shot-shatter problem, and the Germans decided to adopt tungsten as the material to attack tanks. But tungsten is about twice as heavy as steel, and making a full-sized shot of tungsten inevitably meant low velocities which would prevent penetration. The taper-bored gun developed to circumvent this shortcoming, fired a shot that had a tungsten core and a light alloy body capable of being compressed. When the shot was loaded it was of large calibre and light in weight; as it passed down the tapering barrel the alloy was squeezed down until it emerged from the muzzle small in diameter and heavy in relationship to its diameter, which gave it good carrying power and allowed it to keep up its high velocity. The tungsten did not shatter when it struck the tank, but pierced cleanly and then broke up inside to ricochet around and do damage.

slightly, and the problem soon came back again.

In 1938 two mysterious Swiss gentlemen announced to the various military attachés in Switzerland that they had a 'new and powerful explosive' which could penetrate armour. They announced a demonstration, and the military attachés reported back to their masters and arranged for various ammunition experts to attend.

At the demonstration, the Swiss fired rifle-grenades at a sheet of armour and, sure enough, blew holes right through it. They then mentioned large sums of money, and the experts went away to think about it. More than one of the experts realized that what they had been watching was not a new explosive at all but a fairly old idea that had been revived and apparently been made to work by the two Swiss. The idea was called the 'Monroe Effect', because in the 1880s an American experimenter called Monroe had been doing some work on gun-cotton and found that if he laid a slab of gun-cotton on a sheet of steel and fired it nothing much happened to the steel. But if he turned the slab so that the incised letters 'USN' (for the US Navy, who made the gun-cotton) were against the steel, then the letters were reproduced deeply in the surface of the steel. This became something of a parlour trick among explosives scientists, but in spite of some work on it during the 1914-18 war nobody managed to put it to practical use. Now it seemed that the Swiss had done so, and the various experts went back to their own laboratories determined not to be outdone by a pair of amateurs.

The result of their work began to appear late in 1940 as the first 'hollow charge' munitions went into service. The principle of these projectiles — rifle-grenades and artillery shells — was that the nose was hollow, and the body held a charge of high

One of the steel turrets of the fortress of Eben Emael in Belgium which was penetrated with shaped charges.

The British, confronted with the same problem, designed a projectile in pieces, one that had a 'sub-projectile' of tungsten surrounded by a full-bore 'sabot' or support of light alloy. When loaded, the projectile was much lighter than a standard steel shot and so moved off at very high velocity; the construction was such that as it left the muzzle the light alloy sabot would split in pieces and fall away, leaving the sub-projectile to fly to the target. This 'Armour Piercing Discarding Sabot' projectile appeared in 1944 and was to prove the most potent anti-tank weapon of the war. The German design, good as it was, did not survive the grave shortage of tungsten which affected Germany from 1943 onwards; they had the choice: they could use tungsten for machine tools or fire it off in ammunition — and the machine tools won the day.

The search for a suitable anti-tank weapon for infantry was now becoming desperate. The answer seemed to lie with the hollow-charge principle, which relied entirely upon the explosive in the projectile and was independent of range or velocity. The first weapon of this type to appear was the British 'PIAT' or 'Projector, Infantry, Anti-Tank', a weapon that used a novel method of discharging the projectile. Instead of using a barrel, it used a thick steel rod or 'spigot'; the bomb had a long hollow tail, with fins, and the propelling cartridge was inside this tail. The bomb was laid in a trough in front of the spigot; when the trigger was pulled the spigot rod shot into the tail of the bomb and fired the cartridge, and the explosion blew the bomb off the spigot and through the air. The hollow-charge warhead could pierce three inches of armour, enough to deal with most tanks of the time, and the weapon had a range of about 115 metres (125 yards).

By now the Americans had entered the

Above: An Israeli
90mm APFSDS shot.

Two shaped charge projectiles. On the left is the
British 3.7in pack howitzer, developed during
World War II for use against Japanese tanks. On
the right is the PIAT shoulder-fired bomb, the
standard infantry anti-tank weapon of the British
Army from 1942 to 1950.

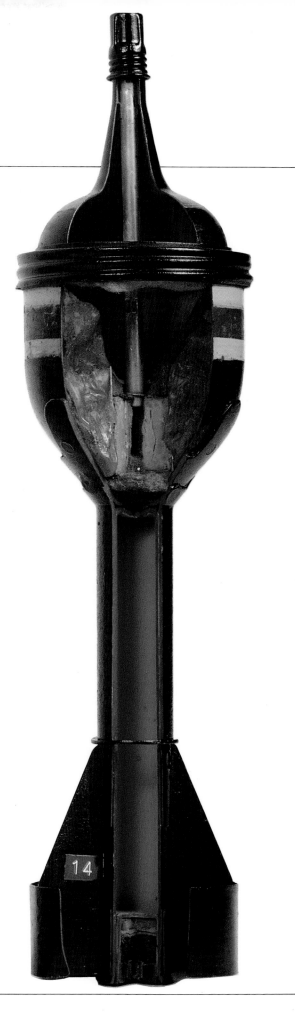

The original American 2.36in bazooka, complete with its shaped-charge rocket.

The 2.36in bazooka in action with the US infantry in Normandy in 1944.

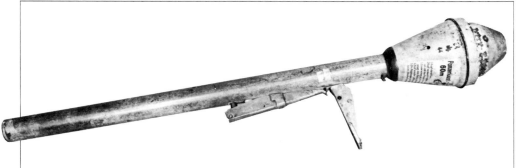

A German *Panzerfaust*. The sight is upright with the trigger behind it. Pressing the rear end down fired the propelling charge and launched the bomb.

war. Their contribution to the infantry's problem took the form of a light tube which a man could place on his shoulder and from it launch a short rocket with a hollow-charge warhead. This was the famous 'Bazooka', which became the principal US anti-tank infantry weapon. Many were given to the Russians, who lost some to the Germans. In no time at all the Germans had their own copy in action, the *Panzerschreck* ('Tank Terror'). But the Germans were not entirely happy with this rather cumbersome weapon, and they devised the *Panzerfaust*, a much smaller tube which could be tucked under the firer's arm and which launched a grenade with a massive hollow-charge warhead.

The *Panzerfaust* was not a rocket; it was among the last of a line of German developments of the recoilless principle. The recoil of a gun had always represented a problem to be overcome, and in major calibres it had meant heavy and complicated hydraulic braking systems on top of heavy and complicated carriages. Dispensing with recoil would remove a great deal of the weight from guns, and this had been the aim of a number of inventors.

The first successful recoilless gun was made by Commander Davis of the US Navy during World War I, and consisted simply of two guns back-to-back. In fact it was a single chamber with two barrels; one held the service projectile, and the other had a similar weight of bird-shot and grease. When the charge was fired in the chamber these two, the shot and the 'counter-shot', went off in opposite directions; both barrels therefore recoiled equally, cancelling out the recoil of each other. The Davis gun was mounted on British Royal Naval Air Service seaplanes as an anti-submarine weapon in 1918, but there is no record of its use in combat.

The Germans applied this countershot idea in a scientific manner. They reasoned that, provided the product of mass and velocity for the shot and countershot were the same, the countershot could be quite light as long as it moved fast enough. The end result was a gun which fired a jet of gas at extremely high velocity through a vent behind the breech block, thus balancing the recoil due to the shell being fired from the barrel. These 'Light Guns' offered 105mm firepower for very little weight and were used to arm German paratroop units. The *Panzerfaust* used the same principle, a small black-powder charge firing the bomb from the front of the tube and exhausting a blast to the rear which counterbalanced the recoil.

Above: A Soviet 82mm recoilless rifle on display at the Warsaw Military Museum.

Below left: Ammunition for a recoilless gun. Note the characteristic perforated case.

Below: A British 105mm light gun firing from a camouflaged position.

The other target worrying soldiers was aircraft. The aeroplane had made great strides since the days of the Zeppelin and was now capable of flying at great speed and altitude. A wide variety of anti-aircraft guns were produced by all the combatants — but the gun was only part of the solution. Finding the target was the major part, solved by the development of radar. The final part was getting the shell to burst as close as possible to the aircraft. The mechanical time fuze had become the standard type of fuze for anti-aircraft fire. It was far more accurate and reliable at high altitudes than the powder-burning fuze but, even so, setting the correct time on the fuze was a matter of educated guesswork. It occurred to some British scientists involved in the development of radar that it might be possible to make a fuze that would pick up the radar energy reflected from the target and react to this when the signal strength indicated that the shell was within striking distance. Tests showed the theory to be correct, but the circuitry and components needed to make it work were far too big to fit inside any projectile. They therefore turned to a new idea, putting a tiny radio transmitter in the fuze, together with a receiver which picked up the reflection of the radio signal from the target and fired the shell when the signal was strong enough. No suitable manufacturing facilities existed in Britain so the idea was passed to the USA in late 1941, together with several other technical secrets. The 'Proximity Fuze' was developed, largely by the Eastman Kodak Company, and first saw service in the Pacific in 1943. It proved invaluable in defending US ships against *kamikaze* suicide aircraft, and it was instrumental in defending Britain against the German flying bomb attacks in 1944.

The Germans, having exhausted most of the possibilities offered by conventional ammunition, moved into a new area when they began to develop guided missiles. As is well known, the 'V-Weapons' did immense damage in Britain and Belgium. The V-1 flying bomb and the V-2 rocket were, however, virtually unguided; they were merely given an initial direction and left to their own devices. But other weapons were further advanced technically. A gliding bomb, steered by radio from the aircraft that dropped it, was used in the Mediterranean in 1943 and sank the Italian battleship *Roma*. Beam-riding anti-aircraft missiles were under development as the war ended, as were tactical ground-to-ground missiles and wire-guided anti-tank missiles.

The lines of development were taken up after the war by the victor nations, and the atomic bomb, developed in USA, was allied with them to produce the fearsome armoury of missiles which now exists. The development of these weapons is largely a matter of electronics and physics, and the ammunition side of the story is relatively conventional; high-explosive warheads for missiles resemble shells in many respects, but their size allows exceptionally complex fuzing and fragmentation control to be achieved.

A modern rifle grenade in position on an assault rifle, ready to be fired.

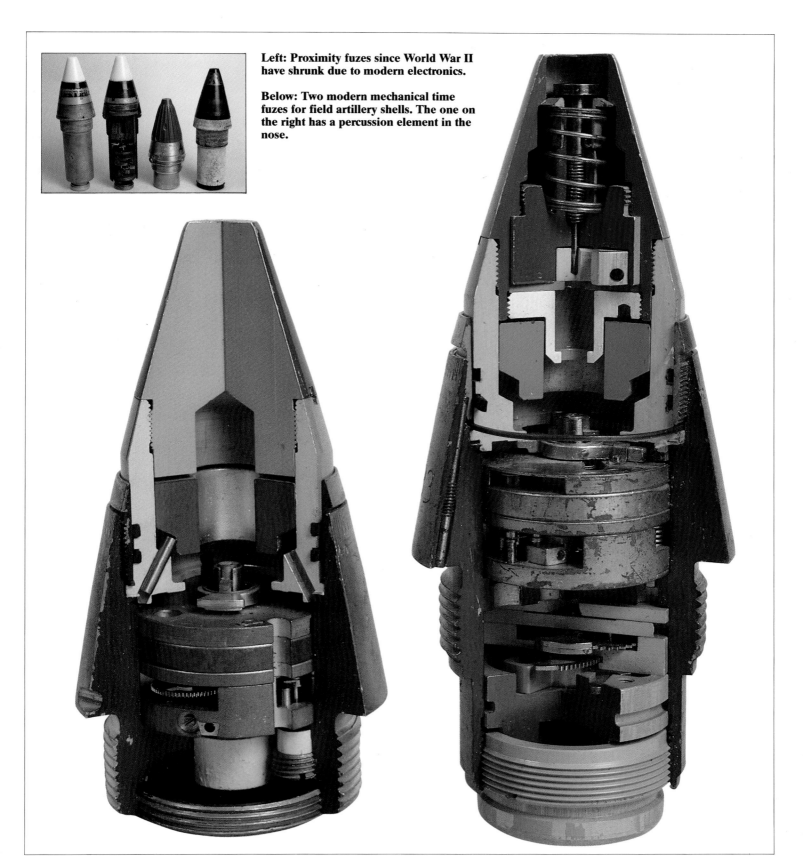

Left: Proximity fuzes since World War II have shrunk due to modern electronics.

Below: Two modern mechanical time fuzes for field artillery shells. The one on the right has a percussion element in the nose.

The British 120mm Wombat recoilless gun fitted with an aiming rifle and image-intensifying night sight.

German ideas for a short cartridge for infantry rifles came to fruition in 1943 with the development of a special 7.92mm cartridge and a new weapon, eventually called an 'assault rifle', to go with it. This development, too was taken up by other countries, and today most major armies are using assault rifles with short cartridges in calibres that would have been thought ridiculous fifty years ago. But, again, this story is really the story of firearms development. The 5.56mm cartridge of today differs only in size from the 7.92mm or .30 cartridge of sixty years ago, and the essential principles remain the same.

In the last five or so years, however, a new dimension has arrived in ammunition, and that is the application of some of the principles of guided weapons to artillery projectiles. In the past the artillery shell was entirely uncontrollable once it left the gun muzzle; today, the use of 'remotely guided munitions' promises some changes in artillery employment. It is now feasible to fire a hollow-charge shell from a howitzer and control the last few seconds of flight so that it strikes a specific target. It is also possible to fire a howitzer shell which bursts above a target area and releases a number of individual 'sub-munitions' which, using

radar techniques, can detect targets and home in on them. Similarly, long-range rockets can be fired to discharge a load of mines in front of an advancing tank force, and once the force has thus been stopped, to bombard them with lethal sub-munitions.

This brief overview of the development of ammunition has of necessity been confined to some of the most important developments. It cannot go into the level of detail on individual items necessary to tell the whole story, but it does fulfil its main objective by showing the general trend of ammunition development.

A Drill version of the Copperhead terminally guided artillery shell — fins spring out after it has left the gun.